Literature and Awareness

An Introduction to the Close Reading of Prose and Verse

Tom Gibbons

GW00385252

Edward Arnold

A division of Hodder & Stoughton

LONDON   MELBOURNE   AUCKLAND

© TOM GIBBONS 1979

First published in Great Britain 1979
Fifth impression 1989

ISBN 0 7131 0314 0

All rights reserved. No part of this publication may be reproduced,
stored in a retrieval system, or transmitted in any form or by any means,
electronic, photocopying, recording, or otherwise, without the prior
permission of Edward Arnold (Publisher) Ltd or a licence permitting
restricted copying. In the United Kingdom such licences are issued
by the Copyright Licensing Agency, 33-34 Alfred Place,
London, WC1E 7DP

Printed in Great Britain by Athenaeum Press Ltd,
Newcastle upon Tyne.

Preface

My aim in writing this short book has been to enhance the reader's experience of literature: to help him or her to read literature with heightened awareness and increased sensitivity, and so to become capable of responding more fully and accurately to the richness and complexity of literary writing in both prose and verse. I have also aimed to familiarize the reader with the most important terms and concepts used in the detailed discussion and exploration of literary writing; to equip him or her, that is, with the basic vocabulary of this branch of literary criticism and appreciation. Although the book is intended primarily for students in schools and universities, I hope that it will help anyone interested in literature towards a greater understanding and enjoyment of literary writing in English.

For students who are preparing for examinations in English literature, I have included exploratory exercises at the end of each chapter. Chapter 8 contains practical advice for students preparing for 'unseen' or 'practical criticism' papers, and includes specimen examples of the detailed discussion and analysis of particular passages of prose and verse.

The present book claims to be no more than a comparatively simple introduction to matters which can be very complex. Its main chapters are devoted to examining particular passages of literary writing in the light of major critical concepts, and further useful terms and concepts are briefly discussed in the Glossary ('Additional Terms'). For those who wish to go further into these matters, more detailed studies by other writers are listed in the section entitled 'Further Reading'. However, one of the simplest ways in which we can get a better grasp of these basic terms and concepts is to realize that they apply not just to literature, but to a large part of our everyday experience.

We are all extremely sensitive to 'diction' and 'tone' in everyday conversation. Newspaper headlines and editorials are full of 'figurative language', advertisements depend heavily upon the 'evaluative connotations' of words, and the letters we receive from bureaucrats are full of 'elevated diction'. 'Irony' and 'bathos' are constantly used in jokes, strip-cartoons in newspapers, television situation-comedies and even television 'commercials'.

In short, the distinctive features encountered in passages of literary writing are everywhere about us, and the more we learn to recognize them in other forms of discourse, the more easily will we be able to recognize them in works of literature.

Most novels, plays and poems express and communicate their authors' *values*. Directly or indirectly, they express and communicate their authors' ideas, opinions and attitudes, especially attitudes of approval and disapproval. They invite us to make moral or ethical discriminations between what their authors regard as comparatively valuable in human experience and what they regard as comparatively worthless. They suggest the desirability or otherwise of our thinking, believing and acting in certain ways.

We can improve our awareness of this aspect of literary writing, too, by becoming more consciously aware of the ways in which various everyday forms of discourse express and communicate values. Most advertisements, newspaper editorials and political speeches are plainly concerned to suggest that certain ways of thinking and behaving are more desirable than others. So, less obviously perhaps, are most run-of-the-mill 'fictions' of all kinds, from a short story in *Woman's Own* to an episode of *Star Trek* (that contemporary morality-play) on television. Careful attention to the strategies employed in these forms of discourse can teach us a great deal about those employed in works of 'serious' literature. And it may, probably will, encourage us to try to work out for ourselves why works of 'serious' literature are themselves so highly valued.

Finally, I should point out that the questions and comments which accompany the passages for discussion at the end of each main chapter are not meant to be either exhaustive or prescriptive. They are intended to provide starting-points for exploration, to suggest some of the many possible ways in which particular passages of literary writing may profitably be approached, thought about and talked about, and to open up wider areas of discussion.

Contents

Acknowledgements

The Publisher's thanks are due to the following for permission to use copyright material:

Baskervilles Investments Ltd., Jonathan Cape Ltd./John Murray (Publishers) Ltd., and Jonathan Clowes Ltd., © Andre Milos, for an extract from Sir Arthur Conan Doyle's *A Study in Scarlet*; the Trustees of the Thomas Hardy Estate, Macmillan, London and Basingstoke (*The Complete Poems: New Wessex Edition*) and Macmillan Publishing Co. Inc. (*Collected Poems of Thomas Hardy*) for Thomas Hardy's 'The Ruined Maid' and 'The Contretemps'; the Executors of the James Joyce Estate, Jonathan Cape Ltd. and Viking Penguin Inc., N.Y., for an extract from James Joyce's 'The Little Cloud' in *Dubliners*; The Bodley Head and © Random House Inc., N.Y. for an extract from James Joyce's *Ulysses*; The Society of Authors on behalf of the Bernard Shaw Estate for an extract from Bernard Shaw's *Man and Superman*; The National Trust for Rudyard Kipling's 'The Bridegroom' and the Estate of the late H. G. Wells for an extract from *Kipps*.

I
Diction

Here and in the various sections of this book which follow, I shall be talking separately about such concepts as 'diction', 'irony', and 'narrative point of view'. It would be a fundamental mistake to think of these as separate *things*, or separable elements, or component parts, of a work of literature (or of an extract from it). They are, it must be insisted, merely *aspects* of a work of literature. Or, better still, they are *concepts*, frames of reference, which we ourselves bring to bear upon works of literature. They exist not so much in the work of literature, like currants in a currant-bun, as in our own minds.

One way of making this clear to ourselves is to start off by remembering that every work of literature is simply a list of words, shorter or longer, in a certain order. This list of words can be looked at from the standpoint of certain useful concepts, such as the concept of 'irony', the concept of 'tone', and so on. But whatever happens, whatever conceptual standpoint we temporarily adopt, we are always and only looking at different aspects of the same list of words.

We may look at an extract from a particular work, let us say a passage from Dickens's *Great Expectations*, from the point of view of its diction or its irony or its tone. But these are not separate parts or elements of the passage. They are merely what we see when we look at the passage with the concept of diction or the concept of irony or the concept of tone foremost in our minds. The tone of the passage does not exist independently of its diction, nor does its irony exist independently of its tone. In other words, the various concepts or frames of reference which we employ when looking at a piece of literature usually overlap each other to a considerable extent.

One useful and important way of studying a particular passage of literature is to begin by examining its diction, or the *kinds* of word of which it is made up. When we speak of 'its' diction here, we really mean its *author's*.

By an author's diction, then, we mean his choice of words, or, more specifically the *kinds* of word which he selects from all the words which are theoretically available to him in the English language.

The words which an author uses are clearly the means by which he communicates his meaning to the reader, and if we can make some general remarks about the kinds of word which he employs, then we have already begun to go some way towards recognizing the particular aspects of reality which interest an author, and which he wishes to single out and comment upon to his reader. The diction of a passage of literary writing, then, is one of the most important of the distinctive features which we ourselves need to be able to recognize and, if necessary, draw attention to and comment on.

In making a general assessment of an author's diction, we may usefully bear in mind such questions as the following: Are the words which the author uses mostly long, or mostly short? Are they mostly derived from Latin, or mostly from Anglosaxon, or from both more or less equally? Are they unusual, even obscure, or are they in common use? Are they formal, or colloquial, or even slangy? Are some of them technical, referring to specialized fields of knowledge such as chemistry, architecture, economics or art? Were they in current use when the author was writing, or were they already archaic? Are they precise, or vague? Are they forceful and energetic, or sober and restrained? Are they concerned with abstract ideas? Are they concerned with states of mind, or feeling? Are they concerned with physical appearances or physical sensations, such as colours, smells, tastes and sounds? Are they evaluative, expressing and inviting approval and/or disapproval? Or are they studiedly neutral?

Is the author's vocabulary large or small? Does he repeat certain words? Does he use clichés; or euphemisms? Does he use words which are more often found in literature or journalism than in everyday speech and writing? Does he use many adjectives, or few? Does he use many adverbs, or few? Does his diction include many active verbs, or perhaps none at all?

Do most of the author's words have only one meaning, in their particular context, or do they have several shades of meaning? Is his diction elevated, or down to earth, or perhaps a mixture of both? These are particularly important questions which will be discussed in the rest of this chapter under the sub-headings of 'Denotation and Connotation' and 'Elevated Diction' respectively.

Two other equally important related questions which we can go on to ask about an author's characteristic choice of words are these: does he use words in their literal senses, by and large, or does he use them *metaphorically*? Does he use words in their literal senses, by and large, or does he use them *ironically*? These questions will be discussed in Chapter 2 ('Figurative Language') and Chapter 4 ('Irony') respectively.

Before going on to the sub-section on 'Denotation and Connotation', the reader might like to examine the following eight sentences, and, bearing in mind the questions suggested above, consider what might be said about the author's diction in each case:

When he saw us come in the door the bartender looked up and then reached over and put the glass covers on the two free-lunch bowls.

There was only the moving to and fro in the moonlight, engrossed, the swinging in the silence, that was marked only by the splash of sheaves, and silence, and a splash of sheaves.

The elegance, propriety, regularity, harmony—and perhaps, above all, the peace and tranquillity of Mansfield, were brought to her remembrance every hour of the day, by the prevalence of every thing opposite to them *here*.

I shall conclude this catalogue of London dainties, with that table-beer, guiltless of hops and malt, vapid and nauseous; much fitter to facilitate the operation of a vomit, than to quench thirst and promote digestion; the tallowy rancid mass, called butter, manufactured with candle-grease and kitchen-stuff; and their fresh eggs, imported from France and Scotland.

Viewed sideways, the closing-line of her lips formed, with almost geometric precision, the curve so well known in the arts of design as the cima-recta, or ogee.

At last, a noble animal was marked down—a ten-foot cattle-killer with a huge roll of loose skin along the belly, glossy-hided, full-frilled about the neck, whiskered, frisky, and young.

In the face of the open gulf, the sun, clear, unclouded, unaltered, plunged into the waters in a grave and untroubled mystery of self-immolation consummated far from all mortal eyes, with an infinite majesty of silence and peace.

It was a modest building, not very straight, not large, not tall; not bold-faced, with great staring windows, but a shy, blinking house, with a conical roof going up into a peak over its garret window of four small panes of glass, like a cocked hat on the head of an elderly gentleman with one eye.

(i) Denotation and Connotation

Is it a distinctive feature of the passage under consideration that many of the words used by its author have only one meaning, in context? Or do many of the words which he uses contain several shades or overtones of meaning? These questions can be conveniently considered in the light of the concepts of 'denotation' and 'connotation'.

The denotation of a word is its basic meaning. Its connotations are its secondary or acquired meanings: what it suggests or implies. The standard example of the difference between 'denotation' and 'connotation' is a good one. It is often pointed out that both the words 'house' and 'home' denote the same thing: a dwelling-place. However, the word 'home' has connotations of comfort, security and family warmth which are lacking in the word 'house'. A song with the refrain 'There's no place like house' would sound singularly flat. The word 'house', on the other hand, *can* have connotations of dignity, long-established reliability and proud family tradition, as when the business firm of Pinchbeck & Co. blossoms forth as The House of Pinchbeck.

In what follows we shall be mainly concerned with the concept of 'connotation'. But it needs to be pointed out first, for the sake of clarity, that large numbers of English words do in fact have several quite different *basic* meanings or denotations. The same word can often be used as a verb or as a noun. Take the word 'dash', for example. This can be used as a verb, meaning amongst other things: 'to shatter' or 'to ruin' (as in 'His hopes were dashed'); 'to rush' (as in 'He dashed away'); or 'to write hastily' (as in 'He dashed off an epic poem'). As a noun, it can mean, amongst other things: 'a sprinkling' ('a dash of salt'); 'a rush' ('a dash for safety'); or even 'a hyphen' (as used in words like 'soda-water'). In practice, we usually have little difficulty in recognizing which denotation of a word is being used, because this is indicated by its context, the words which surround it. The following two captions might appear on the same page of a newspaper: 'Polish City Evacuated'; 'Always Use Our Furniture Polish'. Most of us, it is fairly safe to say, would immediately understand what was meant without even noticing that the same six-letter word was being used in each case.

The *connotations* of a word, as said before, are its secondary or acquired meanings: what it suggests or implies. Take for example the following eight words: 'fluent', 'glib', 'voluble', 'talkative', 'verbose', 'garrulous', 'effusive', and 'loquacious'. All of these adjectives denote more or less the same thing: that the person to whom the term is applied is able to talk easily and at length. The connotations of each word are subtly but definitely different, however. 'Fluent' is usually a term of commendation, while 'talkative' expresses mild disapproval. The other words suggest different kinds and degrees of disapproval. 'Glib' suggests or connotes insincerity, for example, while 'garrulous' suggests wearisome triviality. 'Verbose' suggests pomposity, whilst 'effusive' suggests an embarrassing lack of reserve.

One of the questions about an author's diction which the reader was recommended to bear in mind earlier was this: 'Are the words which the author uses evaluative, expressing and inviting approval and/or disapproval?' It should be apparent from what has just been said about words like 'talkative' and 'garrulous' that the connotations of words play a major part in the expression of an author's evaluations, and in their communication to the reader. Their effect is to shape the reader's responses, very often by the power of suggestion.*

English is a rich language which offers an author a very wide choice of words and of the subtle shades of meaning which they can convey. Certain words (such as the nouns 'rose' or 'key' or 'blood') have acquired an extensive range of possible associated meanings or connotations. As in the case of the possible denotations of a word, it is the context of a word which also indicates which of its particular connotations are being brought into play. This, together with what has so far been said about the general concept of connotation, is best shown by an example. Here are the first four lines of W. B. Yeats's famous sonnet 'Leda and the Swan':

> A sudden blow: the great wings beating still
> Above the staggering girl, her thighs caressed
> By the dark webs, her nape caught in his bill,
> He holds her helpless breast upon his breast.

The rape of Leda by the god Zeus in the form of a swan, which resulted in the birth of Helen of Troy, initiated a cycle of destruction which included the sack of Troy and the murder of Agamemnon by his wife, and which also indirectly produced such great works of literature as Homer's *Iliad* and *Odyssey*, and the *Oresteia* of Aeschylus. Yeats's poem suggests that human beings, like Helen, are merely unwitting instruments of mysterious and perhaps sinister designs initiated by irresistible supernatural forces. The words Yeats chooses, though utterly simple, work strongly to suggest the irresistible and majestic power of the disguised Zeus, the softness and vulnerability of Leda, and the mysterious and possibly sinister pattern of fate in which she is enmeshed by the encounter.

---

* I. A. Richards, in his influential *Principles of Literary Criticism* (1924), distinguished between 'referential language' and 'emotive language'. In Richards's usage, 'referential' language simply denotes, whilst 'emotive' language, through its connotations, expresses and evokes feelings and attitudes.

Although Richards's distinction can be broadly useful, his choice of the word 'emotive' was unfortunate. An established denotation of 'emotive' is 'exciting (or stirring up) emotion (or intense feeling)'. The word is often used to suggest or connote dangerous irrationality, as in the sentence 'His emotive speech lashed his supporters into a frenzy of hatred against all who disagreed with them'. In other words, the term 'emotive language' is itself unavoidably 'emotive' and prejudicial.

For those many words whose connotations are used to express attitudes of approval and disapproval, of different kinds and degrees, I have used the neutral adjective 'evaluative'. Words can be used to express so many different types and shades of feelings and attitudes that all-purpose terms like 'emotive language' are best avoided.

The effects of the connotations of many of Yeats's words become more obvious if we substitute certain other words, as follows:

> A quick thump: the big wings flapping still
> Above the tottering young woman, her upper legs rubbed
> By his murky webbed feet, the back of her neck held by his beak,
> He holds her weak chest against his chest.

What connotations have been removed from the poem by the substitution of words which have the same denotations, but which have quite different overtones? The main ones can be listed as follows: the unexpectedness connoted by 'sudden'; the forcefulness and power connotated by 'blow'; the majesty connoted by 'great'; the controlled power connoted by 'beating'; the uncontrolled reaction connoted by 'staggering'; the defencelessness connoted by 'girl'; the softness and vulnerability connoted by 'nape'; the entrapment connoted by 'caught'. The word 'bill', it should be noted, avoids the connotations of cruelty which might be present in the word 'beak'.

Three pairs of words call for particular attention. 'To caress', in this context, means 'to stroke erotically', so that in the phrase 'her thighs caressed' the possible erotic connotations of the word 'thighs' are brought into play. The phrase 'dark webs' denotes the swan's webbed feet, but 'dark' and 'webs' reinforce each other to produce an extremely complex set of associations which suggest the mysterious, sinister ('dark') and fateful entanglement ('webs') in which Leda is caught up. In the last of the four lines quoted, 'helpless' has connotations of powerlessness and passivity which are absent from 'weak', while 'breast' has connotations of softness, sexuality and physical intimacy which are absent from 'chest'. Taken together, the two words 'helpless breast' also indicate Leda's *feelings of helplessness*. One's physical breast cannot literally be helpless. The word 'helpless' brings into play another of the possible connotations of the word 'breast', namely its use as a term for 'feelings' (the breast being thought of traditionally as an equivalent to the heart, the seat of the emotions). The reader should also note that the word 'swan' already has strong connotations of grace and beauty to begin with. A poem entitled 'Leda and the Duck' would not command much initial respect, presumably.

When Yeats's original lines are compared with my re-written version it can easily be seen that the connotations of his words have the effect, generally speaking, of 'elevating' or dignifying his subject-matter. That is, they invite the reader to think of the coupling of Leda and Zeus as something which is worthy of our most serious attention, something which is momentous and even awe-inspiring. Yeats's diction, then, may be said to be 'elevated'. However, as will be seen in the sub-section which follows (and also in Chapter 7), his elevated diction is extremely restrained when compared with that of some earlier writers.

(ii) Elevated Diction

If elevated diction is a distinctive feature of a passage of literary writing, we need to be able to recognize this and to decide what purpose(s) it serves. As has already been seen in our discussion of Yeats's poem, one important use of elevated diction is to dignify and ennoble the author's subject-matter. In Thomas Gray's famous 'Ode on a Distant Prospect of Eton College' (1747), to take a much earlier example, the poet asks the River Thames which schoolboys now take the lead in such boyish sports as swimming, catching birds, rolling hoops, and playing cricket. These everyday words with their everyday connotations are carefully avoided, however:

> Who foremost now delight to cleave
> With pliant arm thy glassy wave?
> The captive linnet which enthrall?
> What idle progeny succeed
> To chase the rolling circle's speed,
> Or urge the flying ball?

Gray is here dignifying and elevating his subject-matter, as is Alexander Pope in his 'Windsor Forest' (1713). In the following extract, Pope extols the fish to be found in English rivers. Notice how he uses the connotations of such words as 'Tyrian dye' (i.e. crimson), 'silver', 'gold' and 'crimson' to equate the fish with precious metals and the splendid trappings of kings and emperors:

> Our plenteous streams a various race supply,
> The bright-eyed perch with fins of Tyrian dye,
> The silver eel, in shining volumes rolled,
> The yellow carp, in scales bedropped with gold,
> Swift trouts, diversified with crimson stains,
> And pikes, the tyrants of the watery plains.

Diction as elevated as this is no longer fashionable. Yet 'elevation' is continually used today, in both speech and writing, whenever the speaker or writer wishes to invite the serious and respectful attention of his audience. Here for example is a brief extract from a recent speech in which an Australian parliamentarian described an allegedly sinister meeting at sea between a Russian liner carrying Australian passengers, and a Russian submarine and supply-ship:

> Because of darkness and poor visibility, the exact nature of what transpired was unable to be ascertained with any clarity or certainty.

What the speaker wished to say was that it was too dark to see. But he also wished to elevate the importance of the incident, and so used such elevated words as 'visibility', 'transpired', 'ascertained' and 'clarity', together with an elaborately involved sentence-structure. The diction being more impressive than the subject warranted, the effect is one of pompousness, or misplaced elevation. As Pope himself says in his 'Essay on Criticism':

> A vile conceit* in pompous words expressed,
> Is like a clown in regal purple dressed.

This criticism does not necessarily apply to the elevated diction used by Gray and Pope in the examples we have looked at, for Gray's Ode is a meditation on the abiding topics of human suffering and death, while Pope's 'Windsor Forest' is a formal celebration of English life and civilization at their best. Both poems, that is, invite the reader's serious consideration of a topic that is demonstrably serious.

Elevated diction expresses and invites approval (except when it is used ironically, as we shall see in Chapters 4 and 7). As we have already seen in our comments on such words as 'glib' and 'verbose', the connotations of words can also be used to express and invite *dis*approval. Here, for example, is George Orwell's depiction of one of the minor characters in his novel *Nineteen-Eighty-Four*, in which I have italicized the evaluative words whose connotations express disapproval:

> Parsons was Winston's fellow-employee at the Ministry of Truth. He was a *fattish* but active man of paralysing *stupidity*, a *mass* of *imbecile* enthusiasms—one of those completely unquestioning, devoted *drudges* on whom, more than even the Thought Police, the stability of the Party depended. ... An overpowering *smell of sweat*, a sort of unconscious tribute to the strenuousness of his life, followed him about wherever he went, and even remained behind him after he had gone.

Figurative language is often evaluative in much the same way, as will be seen in the chapter which follows.

(iii) Evaluative Diction and 'Character'

'Character' is a matter worth raising here in connection with evaluative diction, because we are often tempted to discuss individual characters

---

* Thought or idea, especially of a far-fetched kind.

in a novel or a play or a poem as if they were real people. This is hardly surprising, as authors work very hard to convince us that their characters *are* real people. So successfully do they do this that we may be tempted to ask such questions as 'What would have happened in *Great Expectations* if Biddy had married Pip instead of Joe Gargery?', or to complain for example that Thackeray is being 'unfair' to Captain Dobbin in *Vanity Fair*. A more sophisticated form of the same naïve way of thinking is apparent when critics of a psycho-analytical turn of mind attempt to psycho-analyze fictional characters (such as Shakespeare's 'Hamlet' or D. H. Lawrence's 'Paul Morel') as if they were real people about whom objective information could be obtained.

All such speculations are in vain, however, because there are no people in a novel or a play or a poem: there are only words. Saying this is a rather forceful way of reminding ourselves that a 'character' can exist in a work of literature only in the manner in which the author presents him to us. The 'character' is no more and no less than the way in which he is depicted. Here for example is Dickens's initial depiction of 'Dennis the Hangman' in *Barnaby Rudge*. I have deliberately chosen an extreme example of the use of evaluative diction here, one in which we experience some difficulty in finding words whose connotations do *not* express disapproval:

> The man who now confronted Gashford, was a squat, thickset personage, with a low, retreating forehead, a coarse shock head of hair, and eyes so small and near together, that his broken nose alone seemed to prevent their meeting and fusing into one of the usual size. A dingy handkerchief twisted like a cord about his neck, left its great veins exposed to view, and they were swollen and starting, as though with gulping down strong passions, malice, and ill-will. His dress was of threadbare velveteen—a faded, rusty, whitened black, like the ashes of a pipe or a coal fire after a day's extinction; discoloured with the soils of many a stale debauch, and reeking yet with pot-house odours. In lieu of buckles at his knees, he wore unequal loops of packthread; and in his grimy hands he held a knotted stick, the knob of which was carved into a rough likeness of his own vile face. Such was the visitor who doffed his three-cornered hat in Gashford's presence, and waited, leering, for his notice.

Much as we might be tempted to, we cannot say that Dickens is describing Dennis unfairly here, because there is no real Dennis to be described, fairly or unfairly: there is no such person. Nor can we even say that Dickens expresses certain attitudes towards him, because there exists no impartially describable Dennis towards whom attitudes of any kind can be expressed.

To say that an author 'describes' a character is not strictly true, either, for it implies that there already exists a character who can be described. It would be more accurate to say that an author 'depicts' or 'presents' a character. And in literature the presentation of a character and the evaluation of 'his' or 'her' personality, attitudes and behaviour go hand in hand. That is, the extended presentation of a 'character' in a novel, poem or play usually carries with it, even *is*, a series of ultimately moral recommendations about the desirability or otherwise of certain kinds of thought and action. Confronted with a character in a work of literature, then, we need to consider why the author should have created an imaginary person along lines which are designed to invite the reader to respond in certain ways: to feel certain degrees of sympathy or antipathy, to approve and/or disapprove of particular aspects of that character's imaginary personality and behaviour.

Instead of asking 'What are the author's attitudes towards this character?' then, perhaps we should ask ourselves 'What moral recommendations is the author making to the reader by *inventing* this character (e.g. 'Hotspur' in Shakespeare's *Henry IV (i)*, or 'Prufrock' in T. S. Eliot's poem, or 'Emma' in Jane Austen's novel)?'

We cannot in fact finally distinguish between 'character' and 'attitudes towards character'. When we try to do so, in this case quite understandably, we are failing to remember that 'character' and 'attitudes' are not separable things which exist *in* the work of literature, but are merely concepts (useful but potentially treacherous) like 'diction' and 'irony'.

Exercise 1

[The Maypole Inn]

When he got to the Maypole, however, and Joe, responding to his well-known hail, came running out to the horse's head, leaving the door open behind him, and disclosing a delicious perspective of warmth and brightness—when the ruddy gleam of the fire, streaming through the old red curtains of the common room, seemed to bring with it, as part of itself, a pleasant hum of voices, and a fragrant odour of steaming grog and rare tobacco, all steeped as it were in the cheerful glow—when the shadows, flitting across the curtains, showed that those inside had risen from their snug seats, and were making room in the snuggest corner (how well he knew that corner!) for the honest locksmith, and a broad glare, suddenly streaming up, bespoke the goodness of the crackling log from which a brilliant train of sparks was doubtless at that moment whirling up the chimney in honour of his coming—when, superadded to these enticements, there stole upon him from the distant kitchen a gentle sound of frying, with a musical clatter of plates and dishes, and a savoury smell that made even the boisterous wind a perfume—Gabriel felt his firmness oozing rapidly away. He tried to look stoically at the tavern, but his features would relax into a look of fondness. He turned his head the other way,

and the cold black country seemed to frown him off, and drive him for a refuge
into its hospitable arms.

Charles Dickens: from Barnaby Rudge

Gabriel Varden, the 'honest locksmith', is determined not to join
his companions in the Maypole on the occasion depicted in the extract.
What kinds of word does Dickens use to present the inn as irresistibly
'hospitable' in his eyes? What do the frequent present participles ('responding', 'running', 'leaving', etc.) contribute to the overall effect?
Which words remind us that we are seeing the inn as Gabriel sees it?
The first sentence of the extract is very long; what do its length and
structure contribute to the overall effect? Is the depiction of Gabriel
sympathetic here? Or is Dickens presenting a character who is to be
condemned for being weak-willed?

Exercise 2

Many apparently simple words have a very large number of possible
denotations and connotations: words like 'free' and 'time', for example,
in Wordsworth's poem below. Something 'calm' may be not only 'still'
but 'quiet', whilst even the word 'with' has complex meanings in a
phrase like 'God be with you'.

What connotations have been removed from Wordsworth's poem
in the re-written version which follows it, which contains words and
phrases of similar denotation but different overtones? What are the
sources and connotations of the phrases 'to lie in Abraham's bosom?'
and 'the inner shrine of the Temple'? What connections are there
between Wordsworth's use of these phrases and his diction? What,
generally speaking, are the effects of Wordsworth's diction here?

It Is a Beauteous Evening

It is a beauteous evening, calm and free,
The holy time is quiet as a Nun
Breathless with adoration; the broad sun
Is sinking down in its tranquility;
The gentleness of heaven broods o'er the Sea:
Listen! the mighty Being is awake,
And doth with his eternal motion make
A sound like thunder—everlastingly.
Dear Child! dear Girl! that walkest with me here,
If thou appear untouched by solemn thought,
Thy nature is not therefore less divine:
Thou liest in Abraham's bosom all the year,
And worship'st at the Temple's inner shrine,
God being with thee when we know it not.

William Wordsworth

It Is a Pretty Gloaming

It is a pretty gloaming, unflustered and at liberty,
The religious duration is noiseless as a cenobite
Out of breath with praying; the extensive sun
Is dropping down in its placidity;
The blandness of the sky rests on the sea:
Hark! the powerful entity is vigilant,
And does with his non-stop shifting make
A thundering din—for keeps.
Precious youngster! precious wench! that strolls with me here.
If you seem unaffected by sober reasoning,
Your character is not consequently less inhuman:
You recline in Abraham's thorax continually,
And attend services at the Church's interior chapel,
The deity being in your company when we are ignorant.

Exercise 3

Pope in his 'Essay on Criticism' comments thus on poems whose authors fall back on clichés (see 'Additional Terms') to provide them with easy rhymes:

Where'er you find 'the cooling western breeze,'
In the next line, it 'whispers through the trees:'
If crystal streams 'with pleasing murmurs creep,'
The reader's threatened (not in vain) with 'sleep'...

Run-of-the-mill fiction also abounds in clichés. Re-write all or part of the following extract, substituting a fresh and original phrase for every cliché that you find; or try to re-write the passage in the style of (say) Dickens or Hemingway.

It was as well that his prairie training had given Jefferson Hope the ears of a lynx. He and his friends had hardly crouched down before the melancholy hooting of a mountain owl was heard within a few yards of them, which was immediately answered by another hoot at a small distance. At the same moment a vague, shadowy figure emerged from the gap for which they had been making, and uttered the plaintive signal cry again, on which a second man appeared out of the obscurity.

'Tomorrow at midnight,' said the first, who appeared to be in authority. 'When the whip-poor-will calls three times.'

'It is well,' returned the other. 'Shall I tell Brother Drebber?'

'Pass it on to him, and from him to the others. Nine to seven!'

'Seven to five!' repeated the other; and the two figures flitted away in different directions. Their concluding words had evidently been some form of sign and countersign. The instant that their footsteps had died away in the distance, Jefferson Hope sprang to his feet, and helping his companions through the gap, led the way across the fields at the top of his speed, supporting and half-carrying the girl when her strength appeared to fail her.

'Hurry on! hurry on!' he gasped from time to time. 'We are through the line of sentinels. Everything depends on speed. Hurry on!'

Once on the high road, they made rapid progress. Only once did they meet anyone, and then they managed to slip into a field, and so avoid recognition. Before reaching the town the hunter branched away into a rugged and narrow footpath which led to the mountains. Two dark, jagged peaks loomed above them through the darkness, and the defile which led between them was the Eagle Canyon in which the horses were awaiting them. With unerring instinct Jefferson Hope picked his way among the great boulders and along the bed of a dried-up watercourse, until he came to the retired corner screened with rocks, where the faithful animals had been picketed. The girl was placed upon the mule, and old Ferrier upon one of the horses, with his money-bag, while Jefferson Hope led the other along the precipitous and dangerous path.

It was a bewildering route for anyone who was not accustomed to face Nature in her wildest moods. On the one side a great crag towered up a thousand feet or more, black, stern, and menacing, with long basaltic columns upon its rugged surface like the ribs of some petrified monster. On the other hand a wild chaos of boulders and debris made all advance impossible. Between the two ran the irregular track, so narrow in places that they had to travel in Indian file, and so rough that only practised riders could have traversed it at all. Yet, in spite of all dangers and difficulties, the hearts of the fugitives were light within them, for every step increased the distance between them and the terrible despotism from which they were flying.

They soon had a proof, however, that they were still within the jurisdiction of the Saints. They had reached the very wildest and most desolate portion of the pass when the girl gave a startled cry, and pointed upwards. On a rock which overlooked the track, showing out dark and plain against the sky, there stood a solitary sentinel. He saw them as soon as they perceived him, and his military challenge of 'Who goes there?' rang through the silent ravine.

Sir Arthur Conan Doyle: from *A Study in Scarlet*

Exercise 4

Virtue

Sweet day, so cool, so calm, so bright,
The bridal of the earth and sky:
The dew shall weep thy fall tonight,
    For thou must die.

Sweet rose, whose hue, angry and brave,
Bids the rash gazer wipe his eye:
Thy root is ever in its grave,
    And thou must die.

Sweet spring, full of sweet days and roses,
A box where sweets compacted lie;
My music shows ye have your closes,
    And all must die.

> Only a sweet and virtuous soul,
> Like seasoned timber, never gives;
> But though the whole world turn to coal,
>   Then chiefly lives.
>
> George Herbert

'Sweets' are perfumes; a 'close' is in one sense the final cadence of a piece of music; the world will 'turn to (char)coal' or be consumed by fire on the Day of Judgement. What does Herbert mean by 'angry', 'ever', 'gives'? Why should the rash gazer 'wipe his eye'?

Herbert's diction is plain, but his use of it is not simple. Both 'music' and 'closes', for example, denote two things simultaneously. Comment on the multiple denotations and connotations of Herbert's diction, paying particular attention to the shifting senses of the word 'sweet' throughout the poem.

Exercise 5

Word-play of all kinds depends upon the variable denotations and connotations of words used in combination (see 'Additional Terms': 'ambiguity').

The poem by Kipling reproduced below, one of a series entitled 'Epitaphs of the War: 1914–18', is addressed to his widow by a young man killed shortly after marriage. Kipling's complex word-play here resembles that of such seventeenth-century poets as Jonson, Herbert and Donne.

Write annotations to the poem, or possibly a full prose version, separating out the various statements which Kipling has fused together by using ambiguous words and phrases.

'Our marriage' is that of the speaker to his 'more ancient bride'; 'Its' refers to 'memory'.

The Bridegroom

> Call me not false, beloved,
>   If, from thy scarce-known breast
> So little time removed,
>   In other arms I rest.
>
> For this more ancient bride,
>   Whom coldly I embrace,
> Was constant at my side
>   Before I saw thy face.

Our marriage, often set—
  By miracle delayed—
At last is consummate,
  And cannot be unmade.

Live, then, whom life shall cure,
  Almost, of memory,
And leave us to endure
  Its immortality.
                Rudyard Kipling

2
Figurative Language

'Does the author use words in their literal senses, by and large, or does he use them *metaphorically*?' In the previous chapter it was suggested that this was a particularly important question to be asked in connection with an author's diction. This related question refers not so much to the author's actual choice of words, as to *how* he uses the words which he has chosen. The author of a letter to a newspaper who writes 'Trades Unions are a cancer which must be cut out of society' is clearly not using the word 'cancer' in a literal sense, but in a metaphoric or 'transferred' sense.

Metaphorical uses of words and phrases are usually included within the wider concept of 'figurative language'. This term, like so many literary terms, is so general and complex that it would be idle to try to find a single unambiguous meaning for it. On balance, it seems a better general term than 'imagery', which is sometimes used in literary discussion to mean much the same thing as 'figurative language'.

'Imagery', however, can also be used to mean any representation of sensory experience, even in literal language. Some authors, such as D. H. Lawrence, often use words which denote physical appearances and physical sensations, and the term 'sensory imagery' can be extremely useful when it comes to describing their manner of writing. Here for example is Robert Browning's two-stanza poem 'Meeting at Night', which is crammed with 'sensory imagery' of this kind:

> The gray sea and the long black land;
> And the yellow half-moon large and low;
> And the startled little waves that leap
> In fiery ringlets from their sleep,
> As I gain the cove with pushing prow,
> And quench its speed i' the slushy sand.
>
> Then a mile of warm sea-scented beach;
> Three fields to cross till a farm appears;
> A tap at the pane, the quick sharp scratch
> And blue spurt of a lighted match,
> And a voice less loud, through its joys and fears,
> Than the two hearts beating each to each!

Conrad is another author who employs a great deal of 'sensory imagery', as may be seen in this extract from his novel *Nostromo*:

Presently Decoud felt a light tremor of the floor and a distant clank of iron. A bright white light appeared, deep in the darkness, growing bigger with a thundering noise. The rolling stock usually kept on the sidings in Rincon was being run back to the yards for safe keeping. Like a mysterious stirring of the darkness behind the headlight of the engine, the train passed in a gust of hollow uproar, by the end of the house, which seemed to vibrate all over in response. And nothing was clearly visible but, on the end of the last flat car, a negro, in white trousers and naked to the waist, swinging a blazing torch incessantly with a circular movement of his bare arm. Decoud did not stir.

Behind him, on the back of the chair from which he had risen, hung his elegant Parisian overcoat, with a pearl-grey silk lining. But when he turned back to come to the table the candlelight fell upon a face that was grimy and scratched. His rosy lips were blackened with heat, the smoke of gun-powder. Dirt and rust tarnished the lustre of his short beard. His shirt collar and cuffs were crumpled; the blue silken tie hung down his breast like a rag; a greasy smudge crossed his white brow.

To avoid confusion, we should probably use the word 'imagery' only as part of the term 'sensory imagery', and adopt the term 'figurative language' for the kinds of use of language discussed in this chapter.

In practice, we need to be able to recognize three kinds of figurative language. We need to be able to recognize when a writer is using words and phrases metaphorically, when he is using the particular kind of metaphor known as 'personification', and when he is using similes. If these are distinctive features of a passage of writing, we need to be able to recognize this fact, and, more importantly, to try to explain to ourselves what part they play in the overall meaning of the passage. It is usually much more important to be able to describe the *effects* of a 'figure of speech' than to be able to decide whether it is a synecdoche or a metonymy.

To be able to recognize when an author is using figurative language is not quite as simple as it sounds, for everyday speech and writing are themselves extremely figurative to begin with. A glance at the dictionary will show that large numbers of words are commonly used in a figurative or transferred sense. The basic meaning of the noun 'star', for example, is 'a celestial body appearing as a point of light'. However, it has also come to mean 'a brilliant actor or actress', while the adjective 'starry-eyed' has come to mean 'romantically and naïvely enthusiastic' (as in the phrase 'starry-eyed idealist'). We say that someone is 'on tenterhooks' without knowing what tenterhooks are (the hooks on which wet cloth is tightened), and we say that someone has been 'hoist with his own petard' without knowing that it means 'blown up by his own bomb'. Newspaper headlines often contain figurative language which passes unnoticed: 'Labour and Liberals Neck-and-Neck in

Latest Poll'; 'Bombshell in Budget Speech'; 'Witch-Hunt in Defence Ministry'. These made-up captions cannot compete, however, with one which actually appeared in an Australian newspaper some years ago: 'Horses to be Guinea-Pigs in Samoa'.

It is to be hoped that any passage of writing which we are studying contains figurative language more original than such examples. As a general rule, a word like 'star' (as in 'John Wayne is a star who usually plays the part of an epic hero') should not be treated as figurative. Where figurative *clichés* are a distinctive feature of a passage of writing, these should certainly be noted.

Here now are some examples of the most important kinds of figurative language which we encounter in passages of literary writing: similes, metaphors, and personifications:

(a) Similes

A simile *states* that one thing is like another. Generally speaking, it makes a comparison between two things which would not normally be regarded as similar to each other.

> As usual, a lot of shaking was required to get him awake. Gwatkin always slept as if under an anaesthetic.
>
> (Anthony Powell)

> Let us go then, you and I
> When the evening is spread out against the sky
> Like a patient etherised upon a table ...
>
> (T. S. Eliot)

> Our moods are apt to bring with them images which succeed each other like the magic-lantern pictures of a doze; and in certain states of dull forlornness Dorothea all her life continued to see the vastness of St. Peter's, the huge bronze canopy, the excited intention in the attitudes and garments of the prophets and evangelists in the mosaics above, and the red drapery which was being hung for Christmas spreading itself everywhere like a disease of the retina.
>
> (George Eliot)

> A touch of cold in the Autumn night—
> I walked abroad,
> And saw the ruddy moon lean over a hedge
> Like a red-faced farmer.
> I did not stop to speak, but nodded,
> And round about were the wistful stars
> With white faces like town children.
>
> (T. E. Hulme)

(b) Metaphors

A metaphor *implies* that one thing is like another. It does this by stating that one thing *is* another. Generally speaking, it makes a comparison between two things which would not normally be thought of as similar to each other.

> The newspaper is the plague, or black death, of the modern world. It is an open sewer, running down each side of the street, and displaying the foulness of every day, day by day, morning and evening.
>
> (Arthur Symons)

> That time of year thou mayest in me behold
> When yellow leaves, or none, or few do hang
> Upon those boughs which shake against the cold,
> Bare ruined choirs, where late the sweet birds sang.
> (William Shakespeare)

> Poor Mr. Casaubon himself was lost among small closets and winding stairs, and in an agitated dimness about the Cabeiri, or in an exposure of other mythologists' ill-considered parallels, easily lost sight of any purpose which had prompted him to these labours. With his taper stuck before him he forgot the absence of windows, and in bitter manuscript remarks on other men's notions about the solar deities, he had become indifferent to the sunlight.
>
> (George Eliot)

(c) Personifications

A personification is a metaphor which attributes human characteristics to non-human things or to abstract qualities. Writers often use similes to do this: in the similes quoted above, the character who is speaking in T. S. Eliot's poem says that the evening is like an anaesthetized patient, while T. E. Hulme says that the stars had white faces like those of town children. However, the term 'personifications' is used for metaphors which state or assume that a non-human thing or quality *is* a person, as in the following examples:

> Madame Life's a piece in bloom,
> Death goes dogging everywhere:
> She's the tenant of the room,
> He's the ruffian on the stair.
> (W. E. Henley)

> There was the large, hard-featured clock on the sideboard, which he used to see bending its figured brows upon him with a savage joy when he was behindhand with his lessons, and which, when it was wound up once a week with an iron handle, used to sound as if it were growling in ferocious anticipation of the miseries into which it would bring him.
>
> (Charles Dickens)

> In misery's darkest caverns known,
>   His useful care was ever nigh,
> Where hopeless anguish pour'd his groan,
> And lonely want retir'd to die.
>   (Samuel Johnson)

I have included the short quotation from Anthony Powell ('Gwatkin always slept as if under an anaesthetic') because it is so unremarkable in comparison with the other examples of figurative language quoted. What it tells us is that Gwatkin always slept as soundly or as heavily as if he were anaesthetized. Although this is a simile in the technical sense of the word, the two things which it compares would normally be regarded as very similar to each other. When we use the term 'figurative language' in literary discussion, we normally have in mind comparisons between two things which have considerably less in common than anaesthetized sleep and heavy sleep of a usual kind, as when the *evening* is likened to an anaesthetized patient in T. S. Eliot's poem. (Eliot's simile suggests that the evening is in a state of suspended animation. The same implied likeness, but in reverse order, is present in the everyday metaphor for mild forms of medical anaesthesia: 'twilight sleep'.)

The other examples of figurative language quoted show something of the vast range of possible similarities which can be stated or implied by writers: mental images are like magic-lantern pictures; red drapery colours the whole field of vision like a disease of the retina; the stars are like town children; newspapers are (like) the Black Death; Shakespeare's advancing years are (like) the coming of winter; poor Mr. Casaubon, lost in his scholarly research is (like) someone lost in a series of underground passages; life is (like) a cheap prostitute (in Henley's poem), and death is (like) her pimp; a clock is (like) a malicious tyrant; anguish is a person who groans, and want (meaning 'poverty') is a person who takes to his death-bed.

The range of possible similarities is so great, and the concept of 'figurative language' is itself so general and complex, that generalizations about the kinds of effect which writers achieve by using figurative language is practically impossible. As with individual words, so with figurative language: everything depends upon the context. But, just as a helpful differentiation can be made between the denotations and connotations of individual words, so a useful differentiation might be made along similar lines between some kinds of figurative use of words and phrases, and other kinds. One might distinguish between figurative language which is used to *explain*, or to clarify, and figurative language which is used to *evaluate*. Many, perhaps most, figuratively used words and phrases do both at the same time, just as most words both denote and connote at the same time.

However, it seems clear that George Eliot likens mental images to magic-lantern pictures primarily to *explain* more clearly what the experience of Dorothea's day-dream was like. On the other hand, Arthur Symons likens newspapers to an open sewer in order to *evaluate* them. He wishes us to think of them as being as loathsome as an open sewer, and to value them accordingly, just as the writer of the letter about Trades Unions wished us to think of them as being as destructive and frightening as cancer, and to value them accordingly.

Figurative language of this kind clearly brings into play some of the strongest of the possible connotations of words like 'sewer' and 'cancer'. It is often used in political argument in order to persuade us to see one thing as if it were another, and to respond, even to act, accordingly. Shakespeare, in the sonnet whose first four lines are quoted above, uses a much more refined and complicated series of metaphors to suggest that his lover should value him and cherish him all the more since the end of his life is in sight.

Metaphors and similes, insofar as they invite us to see things which are unlike as if they *were* alike, have much in common with riddles, which also depend on what appears to be a basic human delight in perceiving unexpected resemblances between things. One might in fact begin a closer examination of the implications and effects of particular similes and metaphors by putting them in the form of a riddle, thus:

Q: Why (in what respects) are the mental images experienced in day-dreams and dozes like magic-lantern pictures?
A: Because they are visual, very vivid, and change very quickly.
Q: Why is the moon in autumn like a farmer?
A: Because it has a big, round, red face and leans over the hedge to stare at the stranger passing by; and because the poem describes a scene in the country.
Q: Why are stars like town children?
A: Because they have white faces, there are lots of them, they are very small, and they are a very long way from the country scene described in the poem.

'Symbol' is a concept which is often included in discussions of figurative language. The term itself has so many different and contradictory meanings that its use is probably best avoided. One possible meaning of the word 'symbol' is worth mentioning here, however, as it helps us to understand metaphors and similes better.

The word 'symbol' has a clear use in sentences such as 'The Eiffel Tower is a symbol of Paris' and 'The kangaroo is a symbol of Australia'.

Here we mean that the Eiffel Tower is something distinctively Parisian that has come to stand for the whole of Paris, and that the kangaroo is something distinctively Australian that has come to stand for the whole of Australia. In other words, both Eiffel Tower and kangaroo have a *representative* status. Each is one example of a wider category of things. It makes sense, then, to say that 'Leda and the Swan' is a symbolic poem, because the coupling of Zeus and Leda is (according to Yeats) one example of the interaction between the divine and the human. It also makes sense, in talking about *The Heart of Darkness*, to say that Conrad's description of the French man-of-war futilely firing its shells into the African jungle is symbolic, for this incident provides one example of 'civilized' man's insignificance in the face of immense natural forces.

A symbol, when the word is used in this sense, claims to be a particular example of a general case. Metaphors and similes, on the other hand, do something entirely different. As we have seen, they invite us to see things which are unalike as if they *were* alike.

Finally, in order to see how evaluative metaphors can be used by writers to shape the reader's responses, let us examine a passage of some length from Chapter 42 of Samuel Butler's famous semi-autobiographical novel *The Way of All Flesh* (1903). The scene to be discussed follows the discovery by his parents that Ernest, a schoolboy, owes a few shillings at various tuck-shops. He is reluctant to explain this debt because he does not want to get either his school-fellows or the friendly and easy-going shopkeepers into trouble with Dr. Skinner, the headmaster.

In presenting this scene Butler likens Ernest's parents, a respectable Church of England clergyman and his highly religious wife, to officials of the Spanish Inquisition, torturing their victim for their own sadistically perverted pleasure while piously pretending that they are doing so for their victim's own good and in the interests of the Christian religion. Whilst forcing Ernest to confess, they pretend that it is *he* who is taking *them* 'into his confidence':

> Then it all came out. He owed this at Mrs. Cross's, and this to Mrs. Jones, and this at the 'Swan and Bottle' public house, to say nothing of another shilling or sixpence or two in other quarters. Nevertheless, Theobald and Christina were not satiated, but rather the more they discovered the greater grew their appetite for discovery; it was their obvious duty to find out everything, for though they might rescue their own darling from this hotbed of iniquity without getting to know more than they knew at present, were there not other papas and mammas with darlings whom also they were bound to rescue if it were possible? What boys, then, owed money to these harpies as well as Ernest?

Here, again, there was a feeble show of resistance, but the thumbscrews were instantly applied, and Ernest, demoralised as he already was, recanted and submitted himself to the powers that were. He told only a little less than he knew or thought he knew. He was examined, re-examined, cross-examined, sent to the retirement of his own bedroom and cross-examined again; the smoking in Mrs Jones' kitchen all came out: which boys smoked and which did not; which boys owed money and, roughly, how much and where; which boys swore and used bad language. Theobald was resolved that this time Ernest should, as he called it, take him into his confidence without reserve, so the school list which went with Dr Skinner's half-yearly bills was brought out, and the most secret character of each boy was gone through *seriatim* by Mr. and Mrs. Pontifex, so far as it was in Ernest's power to give information concerning it, and yet Theobald had on the preceding Sunday preached a less feeble sermon than he commonly preached, upon the horrors of the Inquisition. No matter how awful was the depravity revealed to them, the pair never flinched, but probed and probed, till they were on the point of reaching subjects more delicate than they had yet touched upon. Here Ernest's unconscious self took the matter up and made a resistance to which his conscious self was unequal, by tumbling him off his chair in a fit of fainting.

'The thumbscrews were *instantly* applied ...' There are of course no physical instruments of torture present, though Butler writes as if there were: the 'thumbscrews' are verbal, and Ernest's pain is mental. Nevertheless, Ernest is being tortured, according to Butler, and his respectable Christian middle-class parents are the torturers. The startling and forceful initial metaphor of 'thumbscrews' is sustained and re-inforced by the terms 'recanted', 'examined, re-examined, cross-examined', which suggest the aims and procedures of the Inquisition, and the likeness is later made explicit by the overt reference to 'the horrors of the Inquisition'. To complete the likeness, and to emphasize the unbearable pain of the torture, Butler depicts Ernest as fainting under the ordeal as would a victim of the unbearable physical cruelties of the Inquisition.

The phrases 'probed and probed' and 'touched upon' can be read in such a way as to suggest that the parents are using physical instruments of torture. 'Hotbed of iniquity' and 'awful ... depravity' suggest that they are self-righteously exaggerating Ernest's trivial misdemeanours in order to give themselves an excuse for torturing him. Most importantly, though, the words 'satiated' and 'appetite' suggest that under the guise of 'never flinch(ing)' from carrying out 'their obvious duty' the torturers are in reality taking a perverted pleasure in their work, a suggestion which is re-inforced by the sexual connotations hinted at in the phrase 'subjects more delicate'.

A few pages before the scene we have been looking at, we have been told that Ernest is reluctant to tell his mother what is on his mind because she always betrays his confidences to his father. As Butler puts it, in another startling metaphor: '... the mangled bones of too many murdered confessions were lying whitening round the skirts of his mother's dress, to allow him by any possibility to trust her further'.

Later in the novel, Butler (or rather his narrator, 'Overton') states in passing that 'the long and savage cruelty' with which Ernest had been treated in childhood was 'none the less real for having been due to ignorance and stupidity rather than to deliberate malice'. But Ernest's parents have already been presented to the reader in the likeness of brutal murderers and torturers, as creatures whose malice *is* deliberate. Overton's passing comment, though partly extenuating, is so brief and literal that it does little if anything to undo the impression of Ernest's parents which Butler has already created in the reader's mind by a forceful combination of highly evaluative metaphor and dramatized incident.

The Way of All Flesh has been, and continues to be, a very influential novel, responsible directly or indirectly for the general impression of Victorian middle-class family life held by many people. The satirical figures of Theobald and Christina have been taken to be typical Victorian parents, both in their 'cruelty' to Ernest and their religious hypocrisy. Butler's depiction of them continues to arouse the anger and indignation of readers of his novel; as it was of course designed to do. This in itself is a striking tribute to the power and persuasiveness of figurative language, especially of an evaluative kind.

Exercise 1

[False Eloquence and True Expression]

Words are like leaves; and where they most abound,
Much fruit of sense beneath is rarely found.
False Eloquence, like the prismatic glass,
Its gaudy colours spreads on every place;
The face of Nature we no more survey,
All glares alike, without distinction gay:
But true Expression, like th' unchanging Sun,
Clears, and improves whate'er it shines upon,
It gilds all objects, but it alters none.
Expression is the dress of thought, and still
Appears more decent, as more suitable;
A vile conceit in pompous words expressed,
Is like a clown in regal purple dressed:
For different styles with different subjects sort,
As several garbs with country, town, and court.
                Alexander Pope: from *An Essay on Criticism*

What kinds of figurative language does Pope use in this extract? What different fields of human experience are they derived from? Does Pope use them to explain, or to evaluate, or to do both at once? Would you say that his own writing here was an example of 'false Eloquence', or of 'true Expression'?

The final couplet of the extract deserves particular attention as a summary of the highly important literary doctrine of 'Decorum'. According to this doctrine, diction was to be elevated in exact proportion to the degree of elevation of the subject-matter described, a 'low' word in an epic or tragedy being regarded as a serious breach of decorum. The technique of 'mock-heroic deflation' (see Chapter 7) depends upon an awareness of this principle.

Exercise 2

[Todgers's Commercial Boarding-House]

The top of the house was worthy of notice. There was a sort of terrace on the roof, with posts and fragments of rotten lines, once intended to dry clothes upon; and there were two or three tea-chests out there, full of earth, with forgotten plants in them, like old walking-sticks. Whoever climbed to this observatory, was stunned at first from having knocked his head against the little door in coming out; and after that, was for the moment choked from having looked, perforce, straight down the kitchen chimney; but these two stages over, there were things to gaze at from the top of Todgers's, well worth your seeing too. For first and foremost, if the day were bright, you observed upon the housetops, stretching far away, a long dark path: the shadow of the Monument: and turning round, the tall original was close beside you, with every hair erect upon his golden head, as if the doings of the city frightened him. Then there were steeples, towers, belfries, shining vanes, and masts of ships: a very forest. Gables, housetops, garret-windows, wilderness upon wilderness. Smoke and noise enough for all the world at once.

After the first glance, there were slight features in the midst of this crowd of objects, which sprung out from the mass without any reason, as it were, and took hold of the attention whether the spectator would or no. Thus, the revolving chimney-pots on one great stack of buildings seemed to be turning gravely to each other every now and then, and whispering the result of their separate observation of what was going on below. Others, of a crook-backed shape, appeared to be maliciously holding themselves askew, that they might shut the prospect out and baffle Todgers's. The man who was mending a pen at an upper window over the way, became of paramount importance in the scene, and made a blank in it, ridiculously disproportionate in its extent, when he retired. The gambols of a piece of cloth upon the dyer's pole had far more interest for the moment than all the changing motion of the crowd. Yet even while the looker-on felt angry with himself for this, and wondered how it was, the tumult swelled into a roar; the hosts of objects seemed to thicken and expand a hundredfold; and after gazing round him quite scared, he turned into Todgers's again, much more rapidly than he came out; and ten to one he told M. Todgers afterwards that if he hadn't done so, he would certainly have come into the street by the shortest cut: that is to say, headforemost.

Charles Dickens: from *Martin Chuzzlewit*

What do Dickens's figurative uses of language contribute to the overall effect(s) achieved here? '... Every hair erect upon his golden head' is a figurative reference to the sculpted flames coming out of the gilded urn on top of the Monument, a famous London landmark.

Exercise 3

The Dead

Blow out, you bugles, over the rich Dead!
   There's none of these so lonely and poor of old,
    But, dying, has made us rarer gifts than gold.
These laid the world away; poured out the red
Sweet wine of youth; gave up the years to be
   Of work and joy, and that unhoped serene,
    That men call age; and those who would have been,
Their sons, they gave, their immortality.

Blow, bugles, blow! They brought us, for our dearth,
   Holiness, lacked so long, and Love, and Pain.
Honour has come back, as a king, to earth,
   And paid his subjects with a royal wage;
And Nobleness walks in our ways again;
   And we have come into our heritage.

Rupert Brooke

'But ... has': 'that ... has not'. What are the effects of Brooke's use of the double negative here? Explain his use of 'serene' as a noun. Why does he describe it as 'unhoped (for)'? In what sense(s) would the unborn sons have been the 'immortality' of the dead? What are the connotations of 'heritage' as distinct from 'inheritance'?

A poet writing three years later would probably have begun 'Scream out, you shells, over the gory corpses'. Brooke's sonnet, however, belongs to the early days of the First World War, when there was no thought of military conscription, and many people hoped that the war would re-unite and re-invigorate a nation which they regarded as weakened by moral 'decadence' and civil strife.

Write a detailed description of the effects which Brooke achieves in this poem by using different kinds of figurative language. Compare and contrast his expressed attitudes towards the war with the implied attitudes of Rudyard Kipling in 'The Bridegroom' (p. 14).

Exercise 4

[The Characters of Henry James's Novels]

... The characters, beside being few in number, are constructed on very stingy lines. They are incapable of fun, of rapid motion, of carnality, and of nine-tenths of heroism. Their clothes will not take off, the diseases that ravage them are anonymous, like the sources of their income, their servants are noiseless or resemble themselves, no social explanation of the world we know is possible for them, for there are no stupid people in their world, no barriers of language, and no poor. Even their sensations are limited. They can land in Europe and look at works of art and at each other, but that is all. Maimed creatures can alone breathe in Henry James's pages—maimed yet specialized. They remind one of the exquisite deformities who haunted Egyptian art in the reign of Akhenaton—huge heads and tiny legs, but nevertheless charming. In the following reign they disappear.

Now this drastic curtailment, both of the numbers of human beings and of their attributes, is in the interests of the pattern. The longer James worked, the more convinced he grew that a novel should be a whole—not necessarily geometric like *The Ambassadors*, but it should accrete round a single topic, situation, gesture, which should occupy the characters and provide a plot, and should also fasten up the novel on the outside—catch its scattered statements in a net, make them cohere like a planet, and swing through the skies of memory. A pattern must emerge, and anything that emerged from the pattern must be pruned off as wanton distraction. Who so wanton as human beings? Put Tom Jones or Emma or even Mr. Casaubon into a Henry James book, and the book will burn to ashes, whereas we could put them into one another's books and only cause local inflammation. Only a Henry James character will suit, and though they are not dead—certain selected recesses of experience he explores very well—they are gutted of the common stuff that fills characters in other books, and ourselves. And this castrating is not in the interests of the Kingdom of Heaven, there is no philosophy in the novels, no religion (except an occasional touch of superstition), no prophecy, no benefit for the superhuman at all. It is for the sake of a particular aesthetic effect which is certainly gained, but at this heavy price.

E. M. Forster: from *Aspects of the Novel*

The word 'criticism', as used in the term 'literary criticism', is liable to cause confusion because of its different possible denotations. It can denote, at one extreme, the completely unbiassed investigation of a literary text. At the other extreme it can denote not merely 'the act of passing judgement' but 'deliberate fault-finding'. Perhaps most literary criticism occupies a middle ground between 'explanation' and 'evaluation'?

Forster's comments on James are clearly evaluative. What are his literary values, as expressed in this extract? What part do figurative uses of language play in their expression and communication to the reader? In what sense(s) does he use the word 'wanton'?

Do you think it desirable that literary critics should use figurative language as Forster does here? Do you think that 'characters' in novels should follow his implied prescriptions? Do you agree that James's novels sacrifice 'philosophy' to 'aesthetic effect'?

Exercise 5

[Thackeray, Becky Sharp, and the Reader]

I defy any one to say that our Becky, who has certainly some vices, has not been presented to the public in a perfectly genteel and inoffensive manner. In describing this siren, singing and smiling, coaxing and cajoling, the author, with modest pride, asks his readers all round, has he once forgotten the laws of politeness, and showed the monster's hideous tail above water? No! Those who like may peep down under waves that are pretty transparent, and see it writhing and twirling, diabolically hideous and slimy, flapping amongst bones, or curling round corpses; but above the water-line, I ask, has not everything been proper, agreeable, and decorous, and has any the most squeamish immoralist in Vanity Fair a right to cry fie? When, however, the siren disappears and dives below, down among the dead men, the water of course grows turbid over her, and it is labour lost to look into it ever so curiously. They look pretty enough when they sit upon a rock, twangling their harps and combing their hair, and sing, and beckon to you to come and hold the looking-glass; but when they sink into their native element, depend on it those mermaids are about no good, and we had best not examine the fiendish marine cannibals, revelling and feasting on their wretched pickled victims. And so, when Becky is out of the way, be sure that she is not particularly well employed, and that the less that is said about her doings is in fact the better.

If we were to give a full account of her proceedings during a couple of years that followed after the Curzon Street catastrophe, there might be some reason for people to say this book was improper. The actions of very vain, heartless, pleasure-seeking people are very often improper (as are many of yours, my friend with the grave face and spotless reputation;—but that is merely by the way); and what are those of a woman without faith—or love—or character? And I am inclined to think that there was a period in Mrs. Becky's life, when she was seized, not by remorse, but by a kind of despair, and absolutely neglected her person, and did not even care for her reputation.

This *abattement* and degradation did not take place all at once; it was brought about by degrees, after her calamity, and after many struggles to keep up—as a man who goes overboard hangs on to a spar whilst any hope is left, and then flings it away and goes down, when he finds that struggling is in vain.

W. M. Thackeray: from *Vanity Fair*

Thackeray in *Vanity Fair* is very much the 'intrusive author' (see Chapter 3: 'Narrative Point of View'), addressing his readers directly and often provocatively. His depictions of the adventuress Becky and other characters in the book are deliberately ambivalent in their stated and implied evaluations (see Exercise 4, Chapter 5: 'Tone'). In the extract above he takes a figurative cliché ('siren') and develops it into a complex and forceful 'extended metaphor'.

What do phrases such as 'above the water-line' and 'their native element' suggest about (a) sexual attitudes (b) the structure of society (c) Thackeray's middle-class readers, and (d) the relationships between all three? What does Thackeray's concluding simile contribute to his presentation of Becky here?

3
Narrative Point of View

The concept of 'point of view' is as fundamentally important as the other major concepts discussed in these pages. As a term it is probably the most confusing and the least satisfactory of all, because it mostly has to do, not with seeing, but with *telling*. When we talk about the 'point of view' 'in' a passage of writing, we are actually discussing how the author has chosen to go about telling his story. Although 'point of view' is often an extremely useful term when certain kinds of writing are being discussed, a more sensible *general* term for the whole concept might be 'narrative stance' or even just 'narrative technique'.

The term 'point of view' is also confusing because ambiguous. We use it in an everyday sense as the equivalent of 'attitudes' or 'opinions'; as in the question 'What is your point of view on wage-indexation?', which means 'What are your attitudes towards wage-indexation?' or 'What are your opinions about wage-indexation?'

As we often wish to talk about the points of view put forward by an author in his writing (that is, we wish to discuss his attitudes and opinions), and as the expression of this kind of point of view must often largely depend upon the narrative point of view chosen by the author, the possibilities of confusion are clearly endless. In talking and writing about literature, we would probably do well to use the term 'point of view' only in its technical sense, as having to do with narrative technique, and never to use it in its everyday sense as a substitute for words like 'opinion' or 'attitudes'.

Assuming that every author starts out with some fairly general idea of a story which he wishes to tell, choosing which narrative 'point of view' or 'points of view' to adopt in telling it is clearly one of the first and most fundamental decisions which he has to make. An author's choice of narrative point of view is every bit as important as his choice of words, or diction. We need to be aware of this extremely important aspect of any passage of writing which we may be reading, and to try to ascertain what part it plays in the overall meaning of the passage.

The narrative points of view which are available to an author are almost endless. In what follows, I shall describe and give examples of the basic types of narrative technique which the reader will probably encounter in practice.

One basic choice which an author has is that between 'first-person' narration and 'third-person' narration. In first-person narration, the story-teller usually invents and then impersonates a character who tells his own story 'from his point of view', referring to himself throughout as 'I'. There are numerous first-person novels, such as *Moll Flanders* and *Great Expectations*, and numerous first-person poems, such as the 'dramatic monologues' of Robert Browning and T. S. Eliot. Here are the opening lines of Dickens's first-person novel *Great Expectations* and T. S. Eliot's dramatic monologue 'Gerontion':

> My father's family name being Pirrip, and my Christian name Philip, my infant tongue could make of both names nothing more explicit than Pip. So, I called myself Pip, and came to be called Pip.

> > Here I am, an old man in a dry month,
> > Being read to by a boy, waiting for rain.

It is always dangerous to assume that the invented first-person narrator is voicing the opinions of the author, especially in a dramatic monologue. The exact opposite is very often the case, for the first-person novel or poem gives an author excellent scope for the manoeuvre which I discuss in Chapter 4 ('Irony') under the heading of 'Ironic Impersonation'.

In third-person narration the author does not assume the guise of a fictional character, but remains outside the narrative, referring to the fictional characters in the third person as 'he', 'she', and 'they'. Here are the opening lines of two third-person narratives, R. S. Surtees' novel *Mr. Sponge's Sporting Tour* and the traditional ballad entitled 'The Wife of Usher's Well':

> It was a murky October day that the hero of our tale, Mr. Sponge, or Soapey Sponge as his good-natured friends called him, was seen mizzling along Oxford Street, wending his way to the West.

> > There lived a wife at Usher's Well,
> > And a wealthy wife was she;
> > She had three stout and stalwart sons,
> > And sent them o'er the sea.

In third-person narratives, the author sometimes intervenes to make direct comments to the reader, referring to himself as 'I'. Such authors are known as 'intrusive authors', and we should always be alert to their interventions. Here is a characteristic 'intrusive' comment by George Eliot taken from her novel *Middlemarch*:

> If you think it incredible that to imagine Lydgate as a man of family could cause thrills of satisfaction which had anything to do with the sense that she was in love with him, I will ask you to use your power of comparison a little more effectively,

and consider whether red cloth and epaulets have never had an influence of that sort. Our passions do not live apart in locked chambers ...

The major eighteenth-century and nineteenth-century novelists such as Henry Fielding, Charles Dickens and George Eliot often make intrusive comments of this kind. For what appears to me no very good reason, such comments have been regarded as highly undesirable by some of the best twentieth-century novelists, such as D. H. Lawrence and James Joyce, and one may search their novels almost in vain for direct 'authorial intrusions' of the kind made by George Eliot.

In addition to first-person and third-person narratives, there are a great many poems and novels which employ more than one narrator. Chaucer's *Canterbury Tales* is a series of stories told by a variety of narrators, with linking comments by the third-person narrator, while Browning's long poem *The Ring and the Book* employs a series of first-person narrators who give their own very different accounts of the central incident in which they are all involved. Similar techniques are employed in Wilkie Collins' detective-story *The Moonstone* and in William Faulkner's *As I Lay Dying*.

This last example, which consists of a series of 'direct interior monologues' (see below) may appear at first sight to employ narrative techniques which are startlingly revolutionary. However, it is not very far removed from the so-called 'epistolary novel', or novel written without authorial comment in the form of letters between the characters involved. The use of letters is itself no more than a convention which gives the fictional characters the opportunity to voice their deepest personal feelings and thoughts, as in the twentieth-century 'interior monologue'. Many hundreds of epistolary novels were written during the eighteenth century and early nineteenth century, and the two most famous examples are Tobias Smollett's comic novel *Humphry Clinker* and Samuel Richardson's tragic novel *Clarissa Harlowe*. It would be a mistake to assume that radical experiments in point of view have been carried out only in the twentieth century. Dickens's *Bleak House*, for example, is narrated alternately from two completely different points of view: that of a third-person narrator writing in the present tense, and that of a first-person narrator writing in the past tense.

So far we have been concerned with some of the major choices of narrative point of view which are open to story-tellers. Let us now turn our attention to the most important of the many ways in which the actions, speech and thoughts of characters may be presented in stories.

Actions may be presented in greater or less detail. A scene which might last half an hour in real life may occupy a whole chapter in a novel. On the other hand, the activities of a number of years may be summarized in a few sentences. The same possibilities apply to the presentation of both speech and thoughts.

Speech may be presented in the form of the actual words which the fictional characters are alleged to have spoken. It may be presented as 'direct speech', as in the following example:

> 'You begin to comprehend me, do you?' cried he, turning towards her.
> 'Oh! yes—I understand you perfectly.'

Or it may be presented as 'indirect speech' (or 'reported speech'), which gives the actual words of the characters as they are alleged to have been spoken, but changes the grammatical person of the subject and the grammatical tense of the verb. Here is an example of indirect speech:

> When I told the clerk that I would take a turn in the air while I waited, he advised me to go round the corner and I should come into Smithfield.

This can be converted 'back' into direct speech as follows:

> 'I will take a turn in the air while I wait,' I said to the clerk.
> 'I advise you to go round the corner, and you will come into Smithfield,' he replied.

Again, speech may be presented in the form of summary or paraphrase. The gist of an alleged conversation may be given in a few lines by the author, or it may be given in a still more compressed form:

> A dispute arose on this occasion concerning evidence not very necessary to be related here; after which the surgeon dressed Mr. Joseph's head, still persisting in the imminent danger in which his patient lay ...

It is not unusual to find an author using all three methods of presenting speech (direct speech, indirect speech, and paraphrased speech) in his writing, and even on a single occasion, as in the following extract from *Great Expectations*:

> ... I went into the front office with my little portmanteau in my hand and asked, Was Mr. Jaggers at home?
> 'He is not,' returned the clerk. 'He is in court at present. Am I addressing Mr. Pip?'
> I signified that he was addressing Mr. Pip.

The thoughts of characters may be presented in many different ways, but a useful analogy may be made between the main ways in which speech is presented and the main ways in which thought is presented. Analogous to direct speech is 'direct interior monologue', which presents us with the thoughts of the character exactly as he is alleged to have thought them. The following example, which is taken from James Joyce's *Ulysses*, begins with a sentence by the third-person narrator, and then plunges us into the character's unspoken thoughts:

> As he set foot on O'Connell bridge a puffball of smoke plumed up from the parapet. Brewery barge with export stout. England. Sea air sours it, I heard. Be interesting some day get a pass through Hancock to see the brewery. Regular world in itself. Vats of porter, wonderful. Rats get in too. Drink themselves bloated as big as a collie floating. Dead drunk on porter.

Analogous to indirect speech is the 'narrated interior monologue', in which the actual thoughts of the character are presented, but rendered in the third person and the past tense, as happens in indirect speech. The following example is taken from Joyce's *A Portrait of the Artist as a Young Man:*

> Could it be that he, Stephen Dedalus, had done these things? His conscience sighed in answer. Yes, he had done them, secretly, filthily, time after time, and, hardened in sinful impenitence, he had dared to wear the mask of holiness before the tabernacle itself while his soul within was a living mass of corruption. How came it that God had not struck him dead?

As in the case of indirect speech and direct speech, narrated interior monologue can be converted 'back' into direct interior monologue, as follows:

> Can it be that I, Stephen Dedalus, have done these things? His conscience sighed in answer. Yes, I have done them, secretly, filthily, time after time ...

And so on. Both the direct and the narrated forms of interior monologue, like the first-person novel and the first-person poem (dramatic monologue), lend themselves readily to the manœuvre of Ironic Impersonation. In the case of the narrated interior monologue, however, there is a considerable and consistent danger that the unwary reader will think that the character's thoughts are the author's comments, and consequently misread the book. Both Joyce and Jane Austen (another author who often uses narrated interior monologue, especially in *Emma*) have been disastrously misinterpreted by many readers who are unaware of the narrative point of view which these authors are employing (see Chapters 4 and 7).

Finally, before a very general point is made about the effects of some of these narrative techniques, it should be mentioned that thoughts,

like actions and speeches, can be presented in summaries and para-
phrases of greater or less detail. Here is an example of thoughts presented in a very summary way:

> The prudent waiting-gentlewoman had duly weighed the whole matter, and found,
> on mature deliberation, that a good place in possession was better than one in
> expectation.

*   *   *

The effects which can be achieved through the uses of such techniques, in all their possible permutations and combinations, are as various as the techniques themselves. However, in connection with the
representation of 'character', one very useful general point may be
made about the part likely to be played by an author's chosen narrative
point of view or points of view in a particular passage of writing.

This point is related to the concept of 'distance', which is every bit
as complex and general as most literary concepts. However, in this
brief comment, I wish to say something only about the kind of 'distance' created between the characters in a story and the readers of that
story by the author's choice of narrative point(s) of view. 'Distance',
in this context, refers to the degree of sympathy or antipathy which
the reader is invited to feel towards a particular character or characters.

As a general rule, a detailed and fully developed 'internal' presentation which depicts the fictional character's alleged inner thoughts and
feelings, particularly by means of direct or narrated interior monologues in novels and poems, or soliloquies in plays, is likely to make
the reader sympathize and identify with 'him' or with 'her'. This is
not to say that a sympathetic character cannot be created by means
of 'external' description alone. However, a mainly unsympathetic
character is usually an externally presented one, one whose alleged inner thoughts and feelings we are not allowed to share. Were we allowed
to share the inner thoughts and feelings of the 'villain' in a play or
a novel for example (and to take an extreme case), we would probably
begin to find that 'he' was human like ourselves, with the same human
problems, the same human hesitations, and the same human mixture
of good and bad points in his mental make-up. And then, of course,
he would cease to be the villain.

An instructive example of a change in 'distance' occurs in *Hamlet*
(Act III, scene iii) when the villainous King Claudius is given a soliloquy of his own to speak. Hitherto, we have sympathized and identified
particularly with the character of Hamlet, because he has been allowed

to voice his innermost thoughts and feelings to us directly through his spoken soliloquies. When Claudius voices *his* innermost feelings of guilt and despair, in the soliloquy beginning 'O! my offence is rank ...', we cannot help seeing him for the first time as a suffering human being, and modifying our attitudes accordingly.

It is of course perfectly possible for a highly unsympathetic character to be created 'from the inside'. The inner thoughts and feelings of Browning's fictional monk in 'Soliloquy of the Spanish Cloister' (see Chapter 4) are intended to portray a thoroughly vicious personality, and the commercial traveller Tom Kernan in the 'Wandering Rocks' episode of James Joyce's *Ulysses* is not much better. These, however, are no more than cameos, or miniature portraits, and it seems to be true that a fully-developed interior presentation of character is bound to engage our sympathies, however ironical that presentation may be (as in the case of Jane Austen's 'Emma' and James Joyce's 'Stephen Dedalus').

In considering the effects of an author's choice or choices of narrative point of view in a particular passage, then, the reader should always be particularly alert to the degree of 'distance' which is thereby created between himself and the fictional character(s). As was pointed out in Chapter 1, a 'character' exists only in the way in which the author presents him to us, and the degree of sympathy which we are invited to feel through the control and manipulation of 'distance' plays a highly important part in the moral evaluations of personality and conduct being put forward by the author.

An example of the ways in which this can work in practice will be seen in Chapter 8, in which I compare and contrast passages by Charles Dickens and George Eliot. Meanwhile, it is time to turn our attention to the concept of Irony.

Exercises 1 & 2

We can become more aware of narrative points of view and their fundamental importance, and learn a good deal about the development of the English novel, by comparing and contrasting the works of Henry Fielding (e.g. *Joseph Andrews* and *Tom Jones*) with those of Samuel Richardson (e.g. *Pamela* and, especially, *Clarissa Harlowe*).

These major eighteenth-century novelists differ from each other in nearly every possible way. Fielding's characters are fixed 'types', presented from the outside, and Fielding continually intrudes into his own narrative, making personal comments and drawing attention to his inventing and controlling presence as author. He manipulates distance to produce a comically detached, 'broad' and generalized representation of life and the unchanging varieties of human folly.

Richardson's novels have no narrator in the usual sense. He uses the epistolary form to present his characters from the inside: the letters which make up his novels convey the fluctuating states of mind and feeling of their writers, being written while their 'hearts ... [are] ... wholly engaged in their subjects'. They are also designed to be unconsciously revealing, for according to Richardson styles of writing are 'indicative, generally beyond the power of disguise, of the mind of the writer'. Richardson's minutely detailed 'psychological' representation of life stresses human variety, individuality, complexity and changeability: he is ultimately concerned with the uniquely individual soul and its tragic potential for salvation or damnation.

The two extracts which follow are from Fielding's *Joseph Andrews* and Richardson's enormously long *Clarissa Harlowe*. Describe each author's handling of narrative point(s) of view and the part this plays in shaping the reader's responses.

The passages can be considered separately, or compared and contrasted. A useful way of tackling this question would be to re-write each or both from a different narrative point of view. The episode from *Joseph Andrews* might be re-written as first-person narration (e.g. from Joseph's point of view), and the scene from *Clarissa* re-written as a piece of third-person narration, with or without authorial intrusions. As a *tour de force*, one might try to re-write the extract from *Joseph Andrews* in the manner of Richardson, and the extract from *Clarissa* in the manner of Fielding.

1. from *Joseph Andrews*

The thief who had been knocked down had now recovered himself; and both together fell to belabouring poor Joseph with their sticks, till they were convinced they had put an end to his miserable being: they then stript him entirely naked, threw him into a ditch, and departed with their booty.

The poor wretch, who lay motionless a long time, just began to recover his senses as a stage-coach came by. The postilion, hearing a man's groans, stopt his horses, and told the coachman, He was certain there was a *dead* man lying in the ditch; for he heard him groan. 'Go on, sirrah,' says the coachman; 'we are confounded late, and have no time to look after dead men.' A lady, who heard what the postilion said, and likewise heard the groan, called eagerly to the coachman to stop and see what was the matter. Upon which he bid the postilion alight, and look into the ditch. He did so, and returned, 'That there was a man sitting upright as naked as ever he was born.'—'O J—sus!' cried the lady; 'a naked man! Dear coachman, drive on and leave him.' Upon this the gentlemen got out of the coach; and Joseph begged them to have mercy upon him: for that he had been robbed, and almost

beaten to death. 'Robbed!' cries an old gentleman : 'let us make all the haste imagin-
able, or we shall be robbed too.' A young man who belonged to the law answered,
'He wished they had passed by without taking any notice; but that now they might
be proved to have been *last in his company*; if he should die, they might be called
to some account for his murder. He therefore thought it advisable to save the poor
creature's life, for their own sakes, if possible; at least, if he died, to prevent the
jury's finding *that they fled for it*. He was therefore *of opinion* to take the man into
the coach, and carry him to the next inn.' The lady insisted, 'That he should not
come into the coach. That if they lifted him in, she would herself alight: for she
had rather stay in that place to all eternity than ride with a naked man.' The coachman objected, 'That he could not suffer him to be taken in, unless somebody would
pay a shilling for his carriage the four miles.' Which the two gentlemen refused
to do. But the lawyer, who was afraid of some mischief happening to himself, if
the wretch was left behind in that condition, saying no man could be too cautious
in these matters, and that he remembered very extraordinary cases in the books,
threatened the coachman, and bid him deny taking him up at his peril; for that,
if he died, he should be indicted for his murder; and if he lived, and brought an
action against him, he would willingly take a brief in it. These words had a sensible
effect on the coachman, who was well acquainted with the person who spoke them ;
and the old gentleman above mentioned, thinking the naked man would afford
him frequent opportunities of showing his wit to the lady, offered to join with
the company in giving a mug of beer for his fare; till, partly alarmed by the threats
of the one, and partly by the promises of the other, and being perhaps *a little* moved
with compassion at the poor creature's condition, who stood bleeding and shivering
with the cold, he at length agreed; and Joseph was now advancing to the coach,
where, seeing the lady, who held the sticks of her fan before her eyes, he absolutely
refused, miserable as he was, to enter, unless he was furnished with sufficient covering to prevent giving the least offence to decency. So perfectly modest was this
young man ; such mighty effects had the spotless example of the amiable Pamela,
and the excellent sermons of Mr. Adams, wrought upon him.

Though there were several greatcoats about the coach, it was not easy to get
over this difficulty which Joseph had started. The two gentlemen complained they
were cold, and could not spare a rag; the man of wit saying, with a laugh, 'that
charity began at home'; and the coachman, who had two greatcoats spread under
him, refused to lend either, lest they should be made bloody; the lady's footman
desired to be excused for the same reason, which the lady herself, notwithstanding
her abhorrence of a naked man, approved: and it is more than probable poor
Joseph, who obstinately adhered to his modest resolution, must have perished,
unless the postilion (a lad who hath been since transported for robbing a hen-
roost) had voluntarily stript off a greatcoat, his only garment, at the same time
swearing a great oath (for which he was rebuked by the passengers), 'That he would
rather ride in his shirt all his life than suffer a fellow-creature to lie in so miserable
a condition.'

Joseph, having put on the greatcoat, was lifted into the coach, which now proceeded on its journey. He declared himself almost dead with the cold, which gave
the man of wit an occasion to ask the lady, if she could not accommodate him with
a dram. She answered with some resentment, 'She wondered at his asking her
such a question; but assured him she never tasted any such thing.'

The lawyer was inquiring into the circumstances of the robbery, when the coach stopt, and one of the ruffians, putting a pistol in, demanded their money of the passengers, who readily gave it them; and the lady, in her fright, delivered up a little silver bottle, of about a half-pint size, which the rogue, clapping it to his mouth, and drinking her health, declared, held some of the best Nantes he had ever tasted: this the lady afterwards assured the company was the mistake of her maid, for that she had ordered her to fill the bottle with Hungarywater.

As soon as the fellows were departed, the lawyer, who had, it seems, a case of pistols in the seat of the coach, informed the company, that if it had been daylight, and he could have come at his pistols, he would not have submitted to the robbery; he likewise set forth that he had often met highwaymen when he travelled on horseback, but none ever durst attack him; concluding, that if he had not been more afraid for the lady than for himself, he should not have now parted with his money so easily.

'Pamela': a satirical allusion to the heroine of Richardson's novel, earlier parodied by Fielding in the uproarious *Shamela*. 'Mr. Adams': Parson Adams is Joseph's travelling-companion and moral guide.

What Scriptural episode is alluded to in this extract from Fielding's novel? What purpose(s) does the allusion serve?

2. from *Clarissa Harlowe*

I was in the dining-room before six, expecting her. She opened not her door. I went upstairs and down; and hemmed; and called Will; called Dorcas; threw the doors hard to; but still she opened not her door. Thus till half an hour after eight, fooled I away my time; and then (breakfast ready) I sent Dorcas to request her company.

But I was astonished when (following the wench as she did at the first invitation) I saw her enter dressed all but her gloves, and those and her fan in her hand; in the same moment bidding Dorcas direct Will to get her a chair to the door.

Cruel creature, thought I, to expose me thus to the derision of the women below!

Going abroad, madam?

I am, sir.

I looked cursed silly, I am sure. You will breakfast first, I hope, madam; in a very humble strain; yet with a hundred tenter-hooks in my heart.

Had she given me more notice of her intention, I had perhaps wrought myself up to the frame I was in the day before, and begun my vengeance. And immediately came into my head all the virulence that had been transcribed for me from Miss Howe's letters, and in that letter which I had transcribed myself.

Yes, she would drink one dish; and then laid her gloves and fan in the window just by.

I was perfectly disconcerted. I hemmed, and was going to speak several times; but knew not in what key. Who's modest now, thought I! Who's insolent now! How a tyrant of a woman confounds a bashful man! She was acting Miss Howe, I thought; and I the spiritless Hickman.

At last, I *will* begin, thought I.

She a dish—I a dish.

Sip, her eyes her own, she; like a haughty and imperious sovereign, conscious of dignity, every look a favour.

Sip, like her vassal, I; lips and hands trembling, and not knowing that I sipped or tasted.

I was—I was—I sipped—(drawing in my breath and the liquor together, though I scalded my mouth with it) I was in hopes, madam——

Dorcas came in just then. Dorcas, said she, is a chair gone for?

Damned impertinence, thought I, thus to put me out in my speech! And I was forced to wait for the servant's answer to the insolent mistress's question.

William is gone for one, madam.

This cost me a minute's silence before I could begin again. And then it was with my hopes, and my hopes, and my hopes, and my hopes, that I should have been early admitted to——

What weather is it, Dorcas? said she, as regardless of me as if I had not been present.

A little lowering, madam. The sun is gone in. It was very fine half an hour ago.

I had no patience. Up I rose. Down went the tea-cup, saucer and all. Confound the weather, the sunshine, and the wench! Begone for a devil, when I am speaking to your lady, and have so little opportunity given me.

Up rose the saucy-face, half-frightened; and snatched from the window her gloves and fan.

You must not go, madam!—seizing her hand—by my soul you must not——

Must not, sir! But I must. You can curse your maid in my absence, as well as if I were present—except—except—you intend for *me*, what you direct to *her*.

Dearest creature, you must not go—you must not leave me. Such determined scorn! Such contempts! Questions asked your servant of no meaning but to break in upon me—I cannot bear it!

Detain me not [struggling]. I will not be withheld. I like you not, nor your ways. You sought to quarrel with me yesterday, *for no reason in the world I can think of, but because I was too obliging.* You are an ungrateful man; and I hate you with my whole heart, Mr. Lovelace.

*   *   *

She would have flung from me: I will *not* be detained, Mr. Lovelace. I *will* go out.

Indeed you must not, madam, in this humour. And I placed myself between her and the door. And then, fanning, she threw herself into a chair, her sweet face all crimsoned over with passion.

I cast myself at her feet. Begone, Mr. Lovelace, said she, with a rejecting motion, her fan in her hand; for your own sake leave me! My soul is above thee, man! with both her hands pushing me from her! Urge me not to tell thee, how sincerely I think my soul above thee! Thou hast, in mine, a proud, a too proud heart to contend with! Leave me, and leave me for ever! Thou hast a proud heart to contend with!

Her air, her manner, her voice, were bewitchingly noble, though her words were so severe.

Let me worship an angel, said I, no woman. Forgive me, dearest creature! Creature if you be, forgive me! Forgive my inadvertencies! Forgive my inequalities! Pity my infirmities! Who is equal to my Clarissa?

I trembled between admiration and love; and wrapped my arms about her knees, as she sat. She tried to rise at the moment; but my clasping round her thus ardently, drew her down again; and never was woman more frightened. But free as my clasping emotion might appear to her apprehensive heart, I had not, at the instant, any thought but what reverence inspired. And till she had actually withdrawn [which I permitted under promise of a speedy return, and on her consent to dismiss the chair] all the motions of my heart were as pure as her own.

Lovelace, a rake, has tricked the innocent Clarissa into eloping with him to London. He is keeping her virtually imprisoned in what is, although she does not know it, a brothel. Although he loves her and would be willing to marry her, he prefers to try to seduce her and will eventually rape her.

Miss Howe and Mr. Hickman are other characters in the novel. Dorcas, who acts the part of Clarissa's faithful maid-servant, is really one of Lovelace's many spies. Is her name significant?

Is Richardson's depiction of Lovelace entirely unsympathetic here?

Exercise 3

[Kipps in Love]

The two ladies were standing in the manner of those who have completed their purchases and are waiting for their change. Mrs. Walshingham regarded some remnants with impersonal interest; Helen's eyes searched the shop. They distinctly lit up when they discovered Kipps.

He dropped his hands to the counter by habit, and stood for a moment regarding her awkwardly. What would she do? Would she cut him? She came across the shop to him.

'How are *you*, Mr. Kipps?' she said, in her clear, distinct tones, and she held out her hand.

'Very well, thank you,' said Kipps; 'how are you?'

She said she had been buying some ribbon.

He became aware of Mrs. Walshingham very much surprised. This checked something allusive about the class, and he said instead that he supposed she was glad to be having her holidays now. She said she was, it gave her more time for reading and that sort of thing. He supposed that she would be going abroad, and she thought that perhaps they *would* go to Knocke or Bruges for a time.

Then came a pause, and Kipps' soul surged within him. He wanted to tell her he was leaving and would never see her again. He could find neither words nor voice to say it. The swift seconds passed. The girl in the ribbons was handing Mrs. Walshingham her change. 'Well,' said Miss Walshingham, 'good-bye,' and gave him her hand again.

Kipps bowed over her hand. His manners, his counter manners, were the easiest she had ever seen upon him. She turned to her mother. It was no good now, no good. Her mother! You couldn't say a thing like that before her mother! All was lost but politeness. Kipps rushed for the door. He stood at the door bowing with infinite gravity, and she smiled and nodded as she went out. She saw nothing of the struggle within him, nothing but a gratifying emotion. She smiled like a satisfied goddess as the incense ascends.

Mrs. Walshingham bowed stiffly and a little awkwardly.

He remained holding the door open for some seconds after they had passed out, then rushed suddenly to the back of the 'costume' window to watch them go down the street. His hands tightened on the window rack as he stared. Her mother appeared to be asking discreet questions. Helen's bearing suggested the off-hand replies of a person who found the world a satisfactory place to live in. 'Really, Mumsie, you cannot expect me to cut my own students dead,' she was, in fact, saying....

They vanished round Henderson's corner.

Gone! And he would never see her again—never!

It was as though some one had struck his heart with a whip. Never! Never! Never! And she didn't know! He turned back from the window, and the department, with its two apprentices, was impossible. The whole glaring world was insupportable.

He hesitated, and made a rush, head down, for the cellar that was his Manchester warehouse. Rogers asked him a question that he pretended not to hear.

The Manchester warehouse was a small cellar apart from the general basement of the building, and dimly lit by a small gas flare. He did not turn that up, but rushed for the darkest corner, where, on the lowest shelf, the Sale window-tickets were stored. He drew out the box of these with trembling hands and upset them on the floor, and so, having made himself a justifiable excuse for being on the ground with his head well in the dark, he could let his poor bursting little heart have its way with him for a space.

And there he remained until the cry of 'Kipps! Forward!' summoned him once more to face the world.

H. G. Wells: from *Kipps*

'The class': Kipps, a humble shop-assistant, has been attending an evening-class in wood-carving and has fallen in love with his socially superior and 'artistic' teacher.

Authors can, and do, employ several different narrative points of view in the course of a few pages, or even a few paragraphs.

What explicit remarks and comments does Wells introduce into the scene which he has created? What other points of view does he employ? In what ways do the shifts in narrative point of view contribute to the presentation, sympathetic or otherwise, of the characters depicted?

Exercise 4

[Little Chandler's Reverie]

... He wondered whether he could write a poem to express his idea. Perhaps Gallaher might be able to get it into some London paper for him. Could he write something original? He was not sure what idea he wished to express, but the thought that a poetic moment had touched him took life within him like an infant hope. He stepped onward bravely.

Every step brought him nearer to London, farther from his own sober inartistic life. A light began to tremble on the horizon of his mind. He was not so old—thirty-two. His temperament might be said to be just at the point of maturity. There were so many different moods and impressions that he wished to express in verse. He felt them within him. He tried to weigh his soul to see if it was a poet's soul. Melancholy was the dominant note of his temperament, he thought, but it was a melancholy tempered by recurrences of faith and resignation and simple joy. If he could give expression to it in a book of poems perhaps men would listen. He would never be popular: he saw that. He could not sway the crowd, but he might appeal to a little circle of kindred minds. The English critics, perhaps, would recognize him as one of the Celtic school by reason of the melancholy tone of his poems; besides that, he would put in allusions. He began to invent sentences and phrases from the notice which his book would get. '*Mr Chandler has the gift of easy and graceful verse.*' ... '*A wistful sadness pervades these poems.*' ... '*The Celtic note.*' It was a pity his name was not more Irish-looking. Perhaps it would be better to insert his mother's name before the surname: Thomas Malone Chandler; or better still: T. Malone Chandler. He would speak to Gallaher about it.

He pursued his reverie so ardently that he passed his street and had to turn back.

James Joyce: from *Dubliners*

Little Chandler, the central figure depicted in Joyce's story 'A Little Cloud', is a timid Dublin clerk. Fired by the example of the vulgar journalist Ignatius Gallagher, he begins to dream of a literary career. Like Joyce's 'Stephen Dedalus' later, his aspirations are unmatched by any original talent or creative achievement.

What type of narrative point of view predominates in the extract? What variations in point of view does Joyce employ? What changes in distance are produced by these variations? How do these changes in distance affect our response to the character depicted? What changes in distance take place when the extract is re-written mainly as direct interior monologue?

'Moods and impressions' is a literary cliché of the eighteen-nineties. What other clichés does the extract contain? What are they meant to indicate about the character depicted?

Exercise 5

[Christina's Religious Romanticism]

... Theobald did not feel any call to be a missionary. Christina suggested this to him more than once, and assured him of the unspeakable happiness it would be to her to be the wife of a missionary, and to share his dangers: she and Theobald might even be martyred; of course they would be martyred simultaneously, and martyrdom many years hence as regarded from the arbour in the Rectory garden was not painful, it would ensure them a glorious future in the next world, and at any rate posthumous renown in this—even if they were not miraculously restored to life again—and such things had happened ere now in the case of martyrs. Theobald, however, had not been kindled by Christina's enthusiasm, so she fell back upon the Church of Rome—an enemy more dangerous, if possible, than paganism itself. A combat with Romanism might even yet win for her and Theobald the crown of martyrdom. True, the Church of Rome was tolerably quiet just then, but it was the calm before the storm, of this she was assured, with a conviction deeper than she could have attained by any argument founded upon mere reason.

'We, dearest Theobald,' she exclaimed, 'will be ever faithful. We will stand firm and support one another even in the hour of death itself. God in His mercy may spare us from being burnt alive. He may or may not do so. Oh, Lord' (and she turned her eyes prayerfully to Heaven), 'spare my Theobald, or grant that he may be beheaded.'

'My dearest,' said Theobald gravely, 'do not let us agitate ourselves unduly. If the hour of trial comes we shall be best prepared to meet it by having led a quiet unobtrusive life of self-denial and devotion to God's glory. Such a life let us pray God that it may please Him to enable us to pray that we may lead.'

'Dearest Theobald,' exclaimed Christina, drying the tears that had gathered in her eyes, 'you are always, always right. Let us be self-denying, pure, upright, truthful in word and deed.' She clasped her hands and looked up to Heaven as she spoke.

'Dearest,' rejoined her lover, 'we have ever hitherto endeavoured to be all of these things; we have not been worldly people; let us watch and pray that we may so continue to the end.'

The moon had risen and the arbour was getting damp, so they adjourned further aspirations for a more convenient season. At other times Christina pictured herself and Theobald as braving the scorn of almost every human being in the achievement of some mighty task which should redound to the honour of her Redeemer. She could face anything, for this. But always towards the end of her vision there came a little coronation scene high up in the golden regions of the Heavens, and a diadem was set upon her head by the Son of Man Himself, amid a host of angels and archangels who looked on with envy and admiration—and here even Theobald himself was out of it. If there could be such a thing as the Mammon of Righteousness Christina would have assuredly made friends with it. Her papa and mamma were very estimable people and would in the course of time receive Heavenly Mansions in which they would be exceedingly comfortable; so doubtless would her sisters; so perhaps even might her brothers; but for herself she felt that a higher destiny was preparing, which it was her duty never to lose sight of. The first step towards it would be her marriage with Theobald. In spite, however, of these flights of religious romanticism, Christina was a good-tempered, kindly-natured girl enough, who, if she had married a sensible layman—we will say a hotel-keeper— would have developed into a good landlady and been deservedly popular with her guests.

Samuel Butler: from *The Way of All Flesh*

Read carefully through the extract above, noting Butler's frequent modulations of point of view.

It is not always easy to determine whether a particular sentence is being given from an author's point of view, or from that of one of his characters. Clearly, in the above extract, the middle section is composed entirely of direct speech, while the last sentence of all is composed entirely of authorial comment.

Much of the rest is less clear, however. Most of the first section is presumably paraphrased speech, while most of the last section is paraphrased thought. These narrative points of view in themselves allow an author increased scope for the tendentious presentation of alleged thoughts and utterances (how?). They also allow him to introduce authorial comments unobtrusively, so unobtrusively that the unwary reader may think that the author's comments are the character's thoughts. (We need to keep reminding ourselves here that the thoughts and utterances allegedly being paraphrased are the author's inventions anyway.)

In the first and last paragraphs of the extract, which statements and comments are to be attributed to Christina, and which to the author? Are there any words and phrases which do not clearly belong to either? Why does Butler's depiction of Christina rely so heavily on paraphrased speech and paraphrased thought?

What Scriptural passage is alluded to in the phrase 'Mammon of Righteousness'? What effects does the allusion have?

4
Irony

Irony, if employed in a work of literature, is certainly a distinctive feature which we need to be able to recognize and respond to. Once again, as with the terms 'figurative language' and 'point of view', it should always be remembered that irony is not a thing, but the name given to a concept.

Two major kinds of irony are often distinguished from each other in discussions of this highly important topic: Dramatic (or Situational) Irony, and Verbal Irony. Two other kinds of irony often talked about in connection with literature are Cosmic Irony and Romantic Irony.

These terms, like 'poetry' and 'tragedy', are both sensible and useful. But, like 'poetry' and 'tragedy' they denote concepts of extremely wide application, which it would be vain to attempt a single unambiguous definition of. A particular vice of even sophisticated writers about literature is to try to find a single, all-embracing yet unambiguous definition of irony which will cover the many different kinds of ironical manœuvre employed by authors in the many different genres and sub-genres of literature, from tragedies such as *Macbeth* to satires such as *Gulliver's Travels*.

We begin to move along the right lines, I think, when we put the noun 'irony' on one side for the moment and begin to think in terms of the adjectives 'ironic' and 'ironical'. It is then easier to see that 'ironic' and 'ironical', like most other words, have in fact a wide range of meanings, some of which have scarcely any connection with each other (as was the case with the word 'dash', discussed in Chapter 1).

Instead of trying to find the perfect definition of the term 'Situational Irony', then, let us think rather of the many different kinds of *ironic situation* which authors often contrive for their imaginary characters. And instead of trying to find the perfect definition of the term 'Verbal Irony', let us think rather of the many different kinds of *ironic comment* which authors often make to their readers. It then becomes clear that the word 'ironic' means something considerably different in each case. An 'ironic' situation is, roughly speaking, a 'highly incongruous' situation. An 'ironic' comment, on the other hand, is a comment which is 'not-to-be-taken-at-face-value'.

In what follows I will discuss and give examples of the ironic situations which we are likely to encounter in our reading of literature, and discuss and give examples of the ironic comments which we are also liable to find there. I will also discuss and give examples of a third and equally important 'kind of irony', namely the 'ironic impersonations' which authors often carry out. Here, as applied to the noun 'impersonations', the adjective 'ironic' means something different again. It doesn't mean either 'incongruous' or 'not-to-be-taken-at-face-value'; roughly speaking, it means 'indirectly satirical'.

(i) Ironic Situations

As stated above, an ironic situation is, roughly speaking, a highly incongruous one. Incongruous situations may be of many kinds, but one of the basic and recurring forms of incongruity presented in literature is that between a character's illusions and the reality of which he is unaware. 'Alas, regardless of their doom, the little victims play!' writes Thomas Gray in his 'Ode on a Distant Prospect of Eton College', and this statement might be taken as a model for a whole class of ironic situations to be encountered in literature.

In situations of this kind we as readers or spectators are in possession of vital information which is unavailable to the fictional character or characters. Such characters are deluded by appearances, while we perceive the truth of their situations. Gray's schoolboys, happily playing, are unaware of the hideous misfortunes which adult life has in store for them. Similarly, Agamemnon (in Aeschylus' tragedy) returns home in triumph from the Trojan war, not knowing that his wife is waiting to kill him, just as Duncan praises the charming appearance of Macbeth's castle (*Macbeth*, Act I, scene vi), not knowing that he is about to be murdered once inside it. Again, the builders of the magnificent liner *Titanic* (in Hardy's poem 'The Convergence of the Twain') were unaware that the Fates were at the same time building an equally magnificent iceberg for her to founder on, whilst Oedipus (in Sophocles' *King Oedipus*) is unaware that he himself is the murderer on whom he has pronounced sentence of death.

Is it 'ironic', then, when the stalwart hero of a 'Western' movie rides down the main street of Tombstone on his white horse unaware (unlike us) that he is about to be ambushed by the cattle-baron's hired assassins? Is it 'ironic' when James Bond enters his hotel room unaware (unlike us) that the sinister agent of SMERSH lurks behind the door? Probably not, generally speaking. For (ironically enough) the victims of the ironical situations contrived for them by authors are usually presented as being largely to blame for their own misfortunes. They are presented as being *self-confidently* unaware, too self-deceived and self-satisfied to recognize that they are living in a world of illusion, and the discomfitures devised for them by authors are usually intended as warnings to ourselves, lest we should be similarly self-deluded. It is always a matter for applause when a pompous character, head in air, slips on an unseen banana-skin; but it would be a matter for serious concern if ever the same thing were allowed to happen to our modest and virtuous heroine.

Not all ironic situations are as grim as the ones described so far, of course. Ironic situations abound in comedies as well as tragedies. The characters who fawn over Volpone on his supposed death-bed (in Ben Jonson's comedy) and hand over lavish gifts in the hope of becoming his sole heir, are unaware that he is a perfectly healthy confidence-trickster. Jane Austen's Emma is self-confidently unaware that the odious Mr. Elton loves her, and not her protégée as she fondly imagines. The pompous and pedantic Professor Welch (in Kingsley Amis's novel *Lucky Jim*) is unaware of the highly abusive comments racing through Jim Dixon's mind during their polite academic conversations, just as McCoy, mournfully discussing a friend's death and funeral with Mr. Bloom (in Joyce's *Ulysses*) is naïvely unaware that Bloom's thoughts are really centred on the physical attractions of a young woman across the street.

Comedies, while clearly less grim than tragedies, are not necessarily less moral in their intentions, and the ironic situations devised for their characters by the authors of comedies also usually serve to warn readers and spectators, however light-heartedly, against the dangers of over-confidence and self-deception.

(ii) Ironic Impersonations

The same is broadly speaking true of ironic impersonations, which I have earlier described as being 'indirectly satirical'. I use the word 'indirectly' here because the author does not speak in his own voice on these occasions, but assumes that of an invented character, leaving the reader to infer the criticism which the author usually intends. In ironic impersonations of this kind the invented 'victim' is usually naïvely and self-confidently unaware that in telling his story he has unwittingly revealed his true self: his hypocrisy, his weakness, and his self-confidence in the rightness of his own beliefs even when these are quite contradictory. Ironic impersonations of this kind are not by any means confined to literature: they are the stock-in-trade of such excellent

stage-performers as Barry Humphries (with his famous ironic impersonations of 'Edna Everage' and 'Sandy Stone') and Dick Emery.

Nor are ironic impersonations confined to so-called 'serious' literature. Another excellent popular example of an author's use of ironic
impersonation is the novel *Little Me* (1961) by Patrick Dennis, which
purports to be the intimate memoirs of that great star of stage, screen
and television 'Belle Poitrine'. This fictional, though presumably
representative, narrator presents herself as a warm-hearted, generous,
modest and dedicated 'artiste'. Unintentionally on her part, though
of course intentionally on the part of the author, she reveals herself
to be a ruthless and mercenary woman who has relied on the attractions
of her *belle poitrine* ('beautiful bosom') to make up for her complete
lack of acting ability. Here is a short extract in which the narrator describes her wartime marriage to the young army conscript Fred Poitrine, later to die 'a hero's death' by catching his thumb in the space-
bar of his typewriter (an excellent example of 'bathos'; see Chapter
7):

> Our fourteen days together—a lifetime of bliss in a fortnight's furlough—liter-
> ally flew by. Fearing for the fate of Fred's five thousand dollars in a wicked city
> of cut-purses and pickpockets, I deposited the money in my name at a nearby
> savings bank except for a tiny amount which was needed to replenish my vanished
> wardrobe. Having a good head for practical matters, I saw to it that Fred changed
> his marital status with the army and named little me as beneficiary of his insurance.
> These mundane matters aside, sentiment reigned. I knew but little of the culinary
> arts and eagerly faced the challenge of cooking our own little dinners for two. Fred,
> however, saying that he didn't want me to spoil my soft, white hands, preferred
> to dine out.

Reading between the clichés ('lifetime of bliss', 'wicked city', 'culinary
arts', etc.), we detect that 'little me' shrewdly grabbed all her new
husband's money as quickly as possible while he was still alive, also
calculating that she would be able to collect the insurance-money when
he was killed in action. Her cooking was presumably so appalling that
poor Fred was obliged to dine out in order to eat at all.

Not all novels narrated entirely in the first person employ the
manœuvre of ironic impersonation for the purpose of indirectly satirizing the narrator in this way, and in those which do the implied satirical
comments are usually more complex and less insistent than those in
Patrick Dennis's novel. Some wholly 'first-person' novels which
employ the manœuvre of ironical impersonation satirically are Joyce
Cary's *The Horse's Mouth* and *Herself Surprised*, Erskine Childers'
The Riddle of the Sands (early chapters), Defoe's *Moll Flanders*, Ford

Madox Ford's *The Good Soldier*, Thackeray's *Barry Lyndon*, and H.G.Wells's *The First Men in the Moon*. Swift, especially in his *Gulliver's Travels*, *A Modest Proposal* and *An Argument against Abolishing Christianity*, is the great master of ironic impersonation in English, though not of course a novelist. It should also be mentioned here that an ironical impersonation of the kind which we have been discussing is not necessarily satirical, though it usually is. First-person narrators like 'Belle Poitrine' and 'Moll Flanders' are usually a good deal worse than they imagine themselves to be. Mark Twain's 'Huckleberry Finn' and Dickens's 'Esther Summerson' (in *Bleak House*) are both highly self-critical narrators, and both are, by implication, considerably *better* than they imagine themselves to be.

Here is an episode from Twain's ironic masterpiece *Huckleberry Finn* which will make this clear. Huck has grown very fond of the runaway negro slave Jim, with whom he has shared many adventures on their raft as it journeys down the Mississippi. Nevertheless, he is continually worried by the situation, having been brought up to believe it extremely wicked to help runaway slaves. When two white men ask who is sharing the raft with him he finds that he cannot betray Jim into captivity, and tells them it is a white man:

> '... Is your man white or black?'
> I didn't answer up promptly. I tried to, but the words wouldn't come. I tried for a second or two to brace up and out with it, but I warn't man enough—hadn't the spunk of a rabbit. I see I was weakening; so I just give up trying, and up and says:
> 'He's white.'

*   *   *

> They went off and I got aboard the raft, feeling bad and low, because I knowed very well I had done wrong, and I see it warn't no use for me to try to learn to do right; a body that don't get *started* right when he's little ain't got no show— when the pinch comes there ain't nothing to back him up and keep him to his work, and so he gets beat. Then I thought a minute, and says to myself, hold on; s'pose you'd'a' done right and give Jim up, would you felt better than what you do now? No, says I, I'd feel bad—I'd feel just the same way I do now. Well, then, says I, what's the use you learning to do right when it's troublesome to do right and ain't no trouble to do wrong, and the wages is just the same? I was stuck. I couldn't answer that. So I reckoned I wouldn't bother no more about it, but after this always do whichever come handiest at the time.

Huck blames himself for cowardice and deceit, attributing his failings to his innate wickedness. Baffled about what is right and what is wrong, he tries to shrug the matter off. Unwittingly, though, he reveals his innate decency and goodness: his natural affection for another human being is stronger than the moral code which others have tried to impose upon him. It *is* of course no use at all for Huck 'to try to learn to do right', because he doesn't need to; but he himself is presented as being unaware of this.

In poetry the dramatic monologue, already touched upon in Chapter 3 ('Narrative Point of View'), offers the same scope for the manœuvre of ironic impersonation as does the 'first-person' novel. The narrator of T. S. Eliot's 'Portrait of a Lady', in his efforts to be smart at the expense of a lonely middle-aged woman, unwittingly gives us a highly unflattering portrait of *himself* as a callow and rather callous young man-about-town (hence the title of the poem is itself ironical). The narrator of Robert Burns' famous poem 'Holy Willie's Prayer' unwittingly reveals himself to be a sanctimonious humbug, as does John Betjeman's female narrator in his poem 'In Westminster Abbey'. This middle-class lady's wartime prayer begins as follows:

> Let me take this other glove off
> As the *vox humana* swells,
> And the beauteous fields of Eden
> Bask beneath the Abbey bells.
> Here, where England's statesmen lie,
> Listen to a lady's cry.
>
> Gracious Lord, oh bomb the Germans.
> Spare their women for Thy Sake,
> And if that is not too easy
> We will pardon Thy Mistake.
> But, gracious Lord, whate'er shall be,
> Don't let anyone bomb me.

Religious hypocrisy is also the target of Robert Browning's 'Soliloquy of the Spanish Cloister', in which the monkish narrator's criticisms of Brother Lawrence reveal his own pathological and most un-Christian jealousy. Here are the first and fifth stanzas of Browning's poem. In the first stanza the narrator inwardly rages against Brother Lawrence, who is tending his flowers in the monastery garden (flowers which the narrator sabotages on the quiet). In the fifth stanza his snobbish thoughts about his enemy reveal that he mistakes his own outward shows of religiosity for genuine inner piety:

> Gr-r-r—there go, my heart's abhorrence!
> Water your damned flower-pots, do!
> If hate killed men, Brother Lawrence,
> God's blood, would not mine kill you!

What? your myrtle-bush wants trimming?
  Oh, that rose has prior claims—
Needs its leaden vase filled brimming?
  Hell dry you up with its flames!

              *   *   *

When he finishes refection,
  Knife and fork he never lays
Cross-wise, to my recollection,
  As I do, in Jesu's praise.
I the Trinity illustrate,
  Drinking watered orange-pulp—
In three sips the Arian frustrate;
  While he drains his at one gulp.

Not every dramatic monologue is intended to be satirical, though. The self-critical narrator of Kipling's 'M'Andrew's Hymn', like Huckleberry Finn, unwittingly reveals himself to be a better person than he imagines himself to be. But the dramatic monologue as a form of poetry offers such scope for indirect satire by means of ironic impersonation that it might be wise for us always to assume that such a poem is to some extent satirical unless we can satisfy ourselves that it is not.

Returning now to prose fiction, we see that both the direct interior monologue and the narrated interior monologue also offer considerable scope for indirect satire by means of ironic impersonation, as was also mentioned in Chapter 3. Here first of all are extracts from two direct interior monologues, those of Anse Bundren in William Faulkner's *As I Lay Dying* and Molly Bloom in James Joyce's *Ulysses*:

> It's hard country on man; it's hard. ... Nowhere in this sinful world can an honest, hard-working man profit. It takes them that runs the stores in the towns, doing no sweating, living off them that sweats. It ain't the hard-working man, the farmer. Sometimes I wonder why we keep at it. It's because there is a reward for us above, where they can't take their motors and such. Every man will be equal there and it will be taken from them that have and give to them that have not by the Lord.
>
> But it's a long wait, seems like. ... I am the chosen of the Lord, for who He loveth, so doeth he chastiseth. But I be durn if He don't take some curious ways to show it, seems like.

Faulkner's Mississippi farmer is justifying himself in his unspoken thoughts, just as Belle Poitrine was in her 'memoirs'. As in her case, so in his: the ironic impersonation is contrived in such a way that we can readily see through the character's self-deceptions and recognize the 'true' state of affairs for what it is. Anse is neither honest nor hard-working, but regards the storekeepers in towns (who presumably are) as lazy and dishonest. He amusingly misquotes Scripture to serve his own view of life: 'Unto every one that hath shall be given' is what is really said in St. Matthew's gospel, while 'Whom the Lord loveth he chasteneth' is what is really said in the Old Testament *Book of Hebrews*. Clearly, Anse's notion of Heavenly equality is that he is finally going to get his hands on all the good things worked for by other people during their earthly lifetimes, and he is not above grumbling at the Lord for keeping him waiting for them for such a long time.

Here now, from Molly Bloom's famous interior monologue at the end of James Joyce's *Ulysses*, are two short extracts which appear within about a page of each other:

> ... I dont care what anybody says itd be much better for the world to be governed by the women in it you wouldnt see women going and killing one another and slaughtering when do you ever see women rolling around drunk like they do or gambling every penny they have and losing it on horses yes because a woman whatever she does she knows where to stop ...

> ... they have friends they can talk to weve none either he wants what he wont get or its some woman ready to stick her knife in you I hate that in women no wonder they treat us the way they do we are a dreadful lot of bitches ...

Molly first proclaims the superiority of women to men, and then reverses her position completely. Absolutely certain of the rightness of her own views even when these are quite contradictory, she is self-confidently unaware of her revealing reversal of opinion. Joyce's ironic impersonation invites us first to laugh at her wayward self-assurance, and then perhaps to consider whether we ourselves don't usually believe ourselves to be in the right even when our own views are equally contradictory.

As was said in Chapter 3, the narrative technique of 'narrated interior monologue' presents the actual thoughts of a fictitional character, but in the third person and the past tense. As was also said, there is a considerable danger, when this particular narrative technique is used, that the unwary reader will mistake the character's thoughts for the author's comments, as in the following rather long extract from Jane Austen's *Emma*:

> She was not struck by anything remarkably clever in Miss Smith's conversation, but she found her altogether very engaging—not inconveniently shy, not unwilling to talk—and yet so far from pushing, shewing so proper and becoming a deference, seeming so pleasantly grateful for being admitted to Hartfield, and so artlessly impressed by the appearance of every thing in so superior a style to what she had been used to, that she must have good sense and deserve encouragement. Encouragement should be given. Those soft blue eyes and all those natural graces

should not be wasted on the inferior society of Highbury and its connections. The acquaintance she had already formed were unworthy of her. The friends from whom she had just parted, though very good sort of people, must be doing her harm. They were a family of the name of Martin, whom Emma well knew by character, as renting a large farm of Mr. Knightley, and residing in the parish of Donwell—very creditably she believed—she knew Mr. Knightley thought highly of them—but they must be coarse and unpolished, and very unfit to be the intimates of a girl who wanted only a little more knowledge and elegance to be quite perfect. *She* would notice her; she would improve her; she would detach her from her bad acquaintance, and introduce her into good society; she would form her opinions and her manners. It would be an interesting, and certainly a very kind undertaking; highly becoming her own situation in life, her leisure, and powers.

She was so busy in admiring those soft blue eyes, in talking and listening, and forming all those schemes in the in-betweens, that the evening flew away at a very unusual rate; and the supper-table, which always closed such parties, and for which she had been used to sit and watch the due time, was all set out and ready, and moved towards the fire, before she was aware.

The last sentence of the extract, in which Jane Austen describes events from an authorial point of view, confirms that practically all of the previous paragraph is a presentation of Emma's unspoken thoughts. Emma has a mind which, as Jane Austen goes on to say, is 'delighted with its own ideas'; so much so, that in her self-satisfied reverie she neglects her social obligations to other people as hostess of the occasion. A reader who does not recognize that this paragraph is a narrated interior monologue will also fail to recognize that Jane Austen is carrying out an ironic impersonation, in which Emma unwittingly reveals to us that her charitable intentions are no more than a mask for her sudden ambition to condescend to Miss Smith and to dominate her. In Emma's snobbish mind, for example, Miss Smith's 'proper ... deference' to herself indicates that she 'must have good sense' and therefore 'deserve encouragement'. The patronizing implications of 'deserve' are later re-inforced by Emma's self-congratulatory thought that her decision to 'improve' Miss Smith would be a 'very kind' thing for her to do. In short, while Emma deceives herself into thinking that her motives are altruistic, we can see that they are in fact completely selfish.

Narrated interior monologue can, like first-person narration, be used ironically to present a character as being *better* than he imagines himself to be. Like Huckleberry Finn, the young Ernest in Samuel Butler's *The Way of All Flesh* regards himself as wholly despicable, and Butler uses an ironical manœuvre broadly similar to Twain's in order to criticize the hypocrisy of the boy's moral mentors. The narrative point

of view employed by Butler is much less ambiguous than that
employed by Jane Austen in the passage just discussed, as the following
extract will make clear:

> Ernest, still in Mrs Jay's room, mused onward. 'Grown-up people,' he said to
> himself, 'when they were ladies and gentlemen, never did naughty things, but he
> was always doing them. He had heard that some grown-up people were worldly,
> which of course was wrong, still this was quite distinct from being naughty, and
> did not get them punished or scolded. His own Papa and Mamma were not even
> worldly: they had often explained to him that they were exceptionally unworldly;
> he well knew that they had never done anything naughty since they had been child-
> ren, and that even as children they had been nearly faultless. Oh! how different
> from himself. When should he learn to love his Papa and Mamma as they had
> loved theirs? How could he hope ever to grow up to be as good and wise as they,
> or even tolerably good and wise? Alas! never. It could not be. He did not love
> his Papa and Mamma, in spite of all their goodness both in themselves and to
> him. He hated Papa, and did not like Mamma, and this was what none but a bad
> and ungrateful boy would do after all that had been done for him. Besides he did
> not like Sunday: he did not like anything that was really good; his tastes were
> low and such as he was ashamed of. . . .

Before we go on to consider the topic of 'Ironic Comments', two
final points may be made about ironic impersonation. Firstly: the
letters written by individual characters in epistolary novels (see
Chapter 3) also offer considerable scope for this manœuvre. Secondly:
all literary *parody* is a form of ironic impersonation.

(iii) Ironic Comments

An ironic comment is sometimes defined as one which appears to say
one thing but really implies its opposite, as in the following extract
from Henry Fielding's *Jonathan Wild*:

> . . . If she could ever have listened to the thought of living with any one man, Mr.
> Bagshot was he. Nor was she singular in this inclination, many other young ladies
> being her rivals in this lover, who had all the great and noble qualifications neces-
> sary to form a true gallant, and which nature is seldom so extremely bountiful
> as to indulge to any one person. We will endeavour, however, to describe them
> all with as much exactness as possible. He was then six feet high, had large calves,
> broad shoulders, a ruddy complexion, with brown curled hair, a modest assurance,
> and clean linen. He had indeed, it must be confessed, some small deficiencies to
> counterbalance these heroic qualities, for he was the silliest fellow in the world,
> could neither write nor read, nor had he a single grain or spark of honor, honesty,
> or good-nature in his whole composition.

Clearly, when Fielding describes Mr. Bagshot as having a few small
deficiencies such as absolute stupidity, total illiteracy and complete

viciousness, he does not wish the reader to take him literally. *Jonathan Wild* is a work in which comments *are* to be read in a directly opposite sense to their apparent meaning: the rascally Jonathan Wild is described as 'great' and 'noble' throughout, while the virtuous Thomas Heartfree is presented as an idiot: 'He was possessed of several great weaknesses of mind, being good-natured, friendly, and generous to a great excess.'

Ironic comments in literature are rarely as simple as this, however. An ironic comment always implies something different from what it appears to say, but not necessarily the opposite of what it appears to say. As suggested earlier in this chapter, an ironic comment is one 'which-is-not-to-be-taken-at-face-value'. Here, for example, is the famous ironic opening sentence of Jane Austen's *Pride and Prejudice*:

> It is a truth universally acknowledged, that a single man in possession of a good fortune must be in want of a wife.

We cannot get at the implied sense of this simply by negating one of its verbs, by saying 'must not be', for example, instead of 'must be'. We need to carry out a more complicated 'cancelling-out' operation, which then produces a result along the following lines:

> It is a polite fiction that every wealthy bachelor wants to get married and settle down. The real truth of the matter, which no-one cares to admit, is that every unmarried woman is on the look-out for a rich husband.

Ironic comments are rarely as straightforward as this, however. Take for example Miss Prism's apparently simple remark about her lost novel, in Oscar Wilde's *The Importance of Being Earnest*:

> The good ended happily, and the bad unhappily. That is what Fiction means.

Miss Prism says that literature ('Fiction') shows, and should aim to show, that virtuous people are rewarded and that wicked people are punished.

However, her second sentence can be understood in an entirely different sense, namely: 'That statement is an example of what the word "fiction" (i.e. "untruth") means.' Or, more bluntly: 'That is a good example of a lie.' This second sense, which is of course Wilde's own, undermines Miss Prism's view of literature by pointing out that the earnestly moralistic novels which she and her kind favour are quite untrue to the realities of life as we know them to be: good people often do pretty badly in life, while bad people often do rather well. The type of fiction favoured by Miss Prism is a lie, suggests Wilde. And if we follow his arguments further, we might conclude that such works of literature are therefore immoral, and that the pious opponents of 'immorality' in literature are themselves immoral hypocrites.

By playing on several possible meanings of both 'fiction' and 'means' simultaneously, Wilde has produced a dazzling combination of both 'ironic impersonation' (of Miss Prism and people like her) and 'ironic comment'. Such combinations are far from unusual. In practice, the three basic ironic manœuvres which I have isolated for the purposes of discussion (ironic situations; ironic impersonations; ironic comments) are found in combination more often than not. This being so, and ironic comments being of so many different shades and kinds, I shall now stop talking about ironic comments in isolation, and proceed directly to a detailed examination of two examples of literary writing which contain all three types of basic ironic manœuvre. The first example is Shelley's famous sonnet 'Ozymandias', the second an extract from George Eliot's *Middlemarch*.

(iv) Ironic Manœuvres in Shelley and George Eliot

Ozymandias

I met a traveller from an antique land
Who said: Two vast and trunkless legs of stone
Stand in the desert. Near them, on the sand,
Half sunk, a shattered visage lies, whose frown,
And wrinkled lip, and sneer of cold command,
* Tell that its sculptor well those passions read
Which yet survive, stamped on these lifeless things,
The hand that mocked them and the heart that fed;
And on the pedestal these words appear:
'My name is Ozymandias, king of kings:
Look on my works, ye Mighty, and despair!'
Nothing beside remains. Round the decay
Of that colossal wreck, boundless and bare,
The lone and level sands stretch far away.

The theme of Shelley's poem is a familiar one: the inevitable passing away of earthly power and grandeur. The situation described by the traveller is also an ironic one: Ozymandias had intended that future leaders should look upon his colossal statue and great city, and despair of ever matching his magnificent achievements. However, his statue

---

* Lines 6–8: 'Indicate that its sculptor well understood those passions which still *outlast* ... the sculptor's hand which modelled them and the king's heart which fed them.'

has fallen to pieces and his great city has completely disappeared beneath the desert sands. The inscription on the pedestal is an ironic impersonation of the long-dead king, a device for allowing us to hear his vainglorious words as he 'actually' spoke them long ago. And this ironic impersonation also contains an ironic comment, just as Wilde's ironic impersonation of Miss Prism did. As previously said, Ozymandias had intended that future leaders should read his boastful words and despair of emulating him. Given what has happened to all his achievements, however, the implied meaning of his inscription is now as follows: 'Look what has happened to my triumphs, all you powerful and important people who come after me, and despair, because you can be absolutely certain that all of your achievements will crumble into nothing just like mine'.

In the extract from *Middlemarch* which I shall shortly quote, George Eliot presents the thoughts of Mr. Casaubon, an elderly scholar, during his courtship of Dorothea Brooke, who is many years younger than himself. What the passage 'really' tells us is that Casaubon is utterly self-centred and completely lacking in feeling. He thinks that he *ought* to get married at his time of life, and sees his future wife not as a marriage partner but as a decorative appendage to his own life. Having discovered that he has no strong sexual feelings, he blames everyone but himself. We are left to *infer* all this, however, as George Eliot's overall ironic strategy is one of pretended sympathy for her victim, and agreement with his views. She pretends to follow his line of thought sympathetically, while revealing its essential absurdity. So closely does she follow Mr. Casaubon's line of thought, in fact, and so much of the extract is presented from Mr. Casaubon's point of view, that the narrative technique employed in the passage might for the most part be *almost* described as narrated interior monologue. It is, then, largely an ironic impersonation of Mr Casaubon, and it allows the reader to see the truth of a situation which he is unable to see because of the self-satisfaction and self-delusion which he shares with Belle Poitrine, Anse Bundren and Emma.

Here is the extract, which will be followed by my comments on George Eliot's ironic manœuvres and my own re-writing of the whole passage in non-ironic terms.

> Mr. Casaubon, as might be expected, spent a great deal of his time [visiting Dorothea Brooke] at the Grange in these weeks, and the hindrance which courtship occasioned to the progress of his great work—the Key to all Mythologies—naturally made him look forward the more eagerly to the happy termination of courtship. But he had deliberately incurred the hindrance, having made up his mind that

it was now time for him to adorn his life with the graces of female companionship, to irradiate the gloom which fatigue was apt to hang over the intervals of studious labour with the play of female fancy, and to secure in this, his culminating age, the solace of female tendance for his declining years. Hence he determined to abandon himself to the stream of feeling, and perhaps was surprised to find what an exceedingly shallow rill it was. As in droughty regions baptism by immersion could only be performed symbolically, so Mr Casaubon found that sprinkling was the utmost approach to a plunge which his stream would afford him; and he concluded that the poets had much exaggerated the force of masculine passion. Nevertheless, he observed with pleasure that Miss Brooke showed an ardent submissive affection which promised to fulfil his most agreeable previsions of marriage. It had once or twice crossed his mind that possibly there was some deficiency in Dorothea to account for the moderation of his abandonment; but he was unable to discern the deficiency, or to figure to himself a woman who would have pleased him better; so that there was clearly no reason to fall back upon but the exaggerations of human tradition.

The *situation* which George Eliot has contrived for Mr. Casaubon is of course an ironical one, in the sense of being incongruous. Most people marry *because* of sexual passion, and it is therefore incongruous that Mr. Casaubon, having first of all *decided* to get married, then naïvely expects sexual passion for Dorothea to follow as a consequence. It is still more ironic (incongruous) that he should then blame everyone but himself when the expected passions fail to surge forth.

Many of the author's *comments* are ironical in the sense that they are not to be taken at their face value. They appear to side with Mr. Casaubon, but implicitly emphasize the absurdity of his situation. 'As might be expected' leads us to think at first that Mr. Casaubon is an ardent lover—until we learn that he is really more interested in writing his book than in courting Dorothea. It then becomes clear that the word 'naturally', which appears to mean 'of course', really means 'quite un-naturally'. The cliché 'the happy termination of courtship', which would normally apply to the sexual consummation of marriage, is also being used ironically, because Mr. Casaubon's idea of a happy termination of courtship is in fact to get back to his scholarly research as quickly as he can.

Much of the passage, as has already been pointed out, is given over to an ironical *impersonation* of Mr. Casaubon. Throughout, George Eliot mimics his pompous clichés ('the graces of female companionship'; 'the intervals of studious labour') and his elevated and equally stilted diction ('the solace of female tendance'; 'the moderation of his abandonment').

'The moderation of his abandonment' is a particularly choice example of George Eliot's irony, for we know that wild abandonment is the very last thing that Mr. Casaubon is capable of, and that his term is an ironically self-deluded one for 'total absence of feeling'. Indeed, much of the irony of George Eliot's impersonation depends upon her applying Mr. Casaubon's own scholarly terms of rational calculation to feelings which are generally regarded as sweeping all rational considerations aside. On one hand we have such drily rational words and phrases as 'deliberately', 'made up his mind', 'determined', 'found', 'concluded', 'observed', 'crossed his mind', 'account for', 'discern', 'figure', and 'reason'. And on the other hand we have words and phrases, many of them figurative, which stand for overwhelming sexual feelings: 'abandon', 'stream of feeling', 'immersion', 'utmost', 'plunge', 'passion', and 'abandonment'. These ironies are summed up in the single sentence '. . . he determined to abandon himself . . .', which one might translate, to make the point clearer, as '. . . after much earnest consideration, Mr. Casaubon decided to be wildly passionate . . .'.

If we translate George Eliot's implied satirical comments on Mr. Casaubon into openly satirical ones, and translate her figurative language into non-figurative language, we arrive at the following literal version of the extract:

> Mr. Casaubon, as might be expected, spent a great deal of his time visiting Dorothea at the Grange in these weeks, but this was only because he wanted to get the wedding ceremony over as quickly as possible, so that he could get back to what he foolishly imagined to be his great work—the Key to all Mythologies. However, he calculated that it was worth his while to spare a little time from his research, because he had selfishly decided that he needed a young woman to cheer him up in his off moments, and later to act as a nursemaid when he became really doddery. Ludicrously (given these facts), he had expected to fall passionately in love with Dorothea just because he had decided to marry her, and was amazed to find out that this did not happen! Equally ludicrously, he decided that the reason for this was that the writers of passionate love-poetry had all made love out to be a much more overwhelming experience than it actually was; the real reason, of course, was that he himself was so sexless that he was quite incapable of having any passionate feelings whatsoever. However, he was very pleased with Miss Brooke, because she was exactly the submissive kind of young girl that a completely egocentric old man like himself most needed. He was so absurdly self-satisfied that he often wondered if there was some shortcoming in Dorothea that prevented his being sexually attracted to her; but, despite his efforts, he could not quite make out what her shortcoming actually was, and as she was clearly just the girl he required, he ludicrously decided that the fault could only lie in the fact that mankind throughout the ages had mistakenly attached far too much importance to love and sex.

I said earlier that George Eliot's overall ironic strategy is one of pretended sympathy for her victim. The re-written version makes it clear that not all of her sympathy is pretended, however, for it is very much more severe in its judgements. How has this come about? What has happened, primarily, is that the 'distance' between ourselves and Mr. Casaubon has increased considerably because the element of impersonation has now disappeared.

I said in Chapter 3 ('Narrative Point of View') that 'a fully-developed interior presentation of character is bound to engage our sympathies, however ironical that presentation may be . . .'. George Eliot's presentation of Mr. Casaubon's line of thought is a good example of this. Her ironic impersonation allows us to share his self-delusions from the inside with a degree of sympathy, *and* at the same time to recognize them from the outside for what they really are; which he of course cannot. My re-written version of George Eliot's passage, in presenting Mr. Casaubon entirely from the outside, makes him appear both selfish (which he is, in the original) and calculating (which he is not, in the original). He is in fact not only naïve about marriage but quite oblivious of his own extreme selfishness. Much of Mr. Casaubon's thinking, like Emma's, is devoted to rationalization: to finding high-minded excuses for his own selfishness. George Eliot, like Jane Austen, wishes us to realize that we all resemble Mr. Casaubon in this respect, which we would fail to do if he were distanced from us by a completely exterior presentation such as that in the re-written version.

*   *   *

We need to be able to recognize when an author is employing ironic manœuvres in a passage of writing, and we need to be able to estimate their effects. Neither of these things is easy.

In the first place, ironical comments and ironical impersonations can easily be taken at their face value by the unwary. A coolly ironical letter to a newspaper, recommending for example that all pedestrians should be banned from the centres of our cities because they are getting in the way of motor-cars, is almost certain to call forth an outraged letter to the editor suggesting that it is the motor-cars which should be banned. Swift's *Gulliver's Travels* was in fact mistaken for a genuine account of a real man's voyages by numerous eighteenth-century readers when it was first published, and many readers took entirely seriously 'The Sisters of Tibet', an uproarious satire on Theosophy published by the Victorian novelist Laurence Oliphant in 1884. It is of course particularly ironical that the works of Swift and Jane Austen, who are probably the most sophisticated and relentless ironists in the language, should be regarded as ideal reading for the young and immature.

Our ability to recognize the presence of irony also often depends upon our alertness to the narrative point(s) of view employed by an author, as was pointed out in connection with the extract from *Emma* discussed earlier. To emphasize this point, here is a very short extract from E. M. Forster's *A Passage to India*:

> So peace was restored, and when Adela came to give her evidence the atmosphere was quieter than it had been since the beginning of the trial. Experts were not surprised. There is no stay in your native. He blazes up over a minor point, and has nothing left for the crisis.

It is absolutely essential here to realize that the last two sentences are not Forster's own authorial comments, but a tiny ironic impersonation of the sorts of thing which 'experts' say. Forster is using the word 'experts' ironically, to signify 'self-appointed experts who are far too sure of themselves'.

Against the difficulty of recognizing the presence of irony in works of literature, on the other hand, we may set the indisputable fact that ironic situations, ironic comments and ironic impersonations are by no means confined to literature, but are part and parcel of our everyday experience. Anyone who gets through even one day of his or her life without hearing or making an ironic comment, without being involved in or being made aware of an ironical situation, or without carrying out or witnessing an ironical impersonation of someone else, is presumably living in solitary confinement. Ironic manœuvres are constantly used in strip-cartoons, in films, and on television, where most people seem to have no difficulty in responding to them. The more we learn *consciously* to recognize ironic manœuvres in everyday discourse and the mass media, then, the more easily will we be able to recognize them in passages of literary writing.

Having recognized the presence of ironical manœuvres, we are still left with the difficult task of explaining their effects. One way of putting ourselves in a position to do this, as we saw in connection with the passage from *Middlemarch*, is to write out a literal version for purposes of comparison. There, as we also saw, the effects were to produce a part-sympathetic and part-critical presentation of Mr. Casaubon's personality. Not all ironic manœuvres have these particular effects, of course. In fact, the range of effects obtainable by ironic manœuvres is so great that one cannot sensibly generalize about them. As A. E. Dyson says in his excellent book *The Crazy Fabric: Essays in Irony*:

> No two ironists are wholly alike, whether in their temperament, their background, or their creative manipulation of words. For the critic only very close attention will suffice, to local nuances of tone, as well as to the structure of the whole.

Very broadly speaking, however, it seems to be true that the many kinds of ironic comments, ironic situations and ironic impersonations created by authors do have something in common after all: by and large they are moral stratagems for encouraging us not to be deceived by appearances, and for making us more aware of our all-too-human capacity for self-deception, self-satisfaction, and self-righteousness.

'Tone', mentioned by A. E. Dyson in the quotation above, is an important concept which will be discussed in the chapter which follows.

Exercise 1

The extract below is from Pope's ironic eulogy of the *Pastorals* of Ambrose Philips (the original 'Namby Pamby'). After comparing his own pastoral poems with those of Philips, Pope continues as follows:

> Having now shown some parts, in which these two writers may be compared, it is a justice I owe to Mr. Philips to discover those in which no man can compare with him. First, That beautiful rusticity, of which I shall only produce two instances out of a hundred not yet quoted:
>
> > O woful day! O day of woe! quoth he,
> > And woful I, who live the day to see!
>
> The simplicity of diction, the melancholy flowing of the numbers, the solemnity of the sound, and the easy turn of the words in this Dirge (to make use of our author's expression) are extremely elegant.
>
> In another of his pastorals, a shepherd utters a Dirge not much inferior to the former, in the following lines:
>
> > Ah me the while! ah me! the luckless day,
> > Ah luckless lad! the rather might I say;
> > Ah silly I! more silly than my sheep,
> > Which on the flowery plains I once did keep.
>
> How he still charms the ear with these artful repetitions of the epithets: and how significant is the last verse! I defy the most common reader to repeat them, without feeling some motions of compassion.

'Discover' means 'reveal'; a poet's 'numbers' are his 'versification' or 'skill in handling metre'; 'the last verse' is of course 'the last *line*'.

As a preliminary to describing the ironic manœuvres employed by Pope here, write out a literal version of the extract.

Exercise 2

The Ruined Maid
'O 'MELIA, my dear, this does everything crown!
Who could have supposed I should meet you in Town?
And whence such fair garments, such prosperi-ty?'—
'O didn't you know I'd been ruined' said she.

—'You left us in tatters, without shoes or socks,
Tired of digging potatoes, and spudding up docks;
And now you've gay bracelets and bright feathers three!'—
'Yes: that's how we dress when we're ruined,' said she.

—'At home in the barton you said "thee" and "thou",
And "thik oon", and "theäs oon", and "t'other"; but now
Your talking quite fits 'ee for high compa-ny!'—
'Some polish is gained with one's ruin,' said she.

—'Your hands were like paws then, your face blue and bleak
But now I'm bewitched by your delicate cheek,
And your little gloves fit as on any la-dy!'—
'We never do work when we're ruined,' said she.

—'You used to call home-life a hag-ridden dream,
And you'd sigh, and you'd sock; but at present you seem
To know not of megrims or melancho-ly!'—
'True. One's pretty lively when ruined,' said she.

—'I wish I had feathers, a fine sweeping gown,
And a delicate face, and could strut about Town!'—
'My dear—a raw country girl, such as you be,
Cannot quite expect that. You ain't ruined,' said she.

Thomas Hardy

'Ruined' is a euphemism or polite word for 'deflowered'. The 'ruined maid' is a stock figure of ballad, folk-lore and melodrama, intended as a warning to young virgins. By allowing herself to be sexually 'ruined' by a false lover, she is inexorably doomed to be 'ruined' in every way: deserted, disgraced, forced to leave home with an illegitimate child, she will end up as a suicide, a prostitute, or the inmate of a workhouse. The term itself is a literary and moral cliché.

What attitudes does Hardy invite us to take up towards the view of life and the sexual code (i.e. the values) which are implicit in this cliché? What ironic manœuvres does he use in the poem, and with what effects? Notice that the poem consists entirely of dialogue and contains no comments or statements by a narrator.

One might begin here by considering the various connotations of the word 'ruined' which are brought successively into play by the contexts provided for it by 'fair', 'prosperity', 'gay', 'bright' and other words spoken by the 'raw country girl'. (What are the connotations of 'raw' here?)

We may infer (correctly?) that the 'ruined maid' is hardly as sophisticated in dress or speech as the bedazzled 'raw country girl' imagines. How does this affect our reading of the poem?

Does the 'ruined maid' use the word 'ruined' ironically?

Exercise 3

The Latest Decalogue

Thou shalt have one God only; who
Would be at the expense of two?
No graven images may be
Worshipped, except the currency:
Swear not at all; for for thy curse
Thine enemy is none the worse:
At church on Sunday to attend
Will serve to keep the world thy friend:
Honour thy parents; that is, all
From whom advancement may befall:
Thou shalt not kill; but needst not strive
Officiously to keep alive:
Do not adultery commit;
Advantage rarely comes of it:
Thou shalt not steal; an empty feat,
When it's so lucrative to cheat:
Bear not false witness; let the lie
Have time on its own wings to fly:
Thou shalt not covet; but tradition
Approves all forms of competition.

The sum of all is, thou shalt love,
If any body, God above:
At any rate shall never labour
More than thyself to love thy neighbour.
                    Arthur Hugh Clough

'To keep alive': 'To keep [another person] alive'. '*More* than thyself,
etc.': 'To love thy neighbour *more* than thyself'.

'Thou shalt have one God only, because it's cheaper than having
two of them.' A number of Clough's latter-day Commandments rely
upon an implied 'because'. Which?

Clough's Commandments are not 'comments' in the usual sense,
though clearly they are ironic in that they are 'not to be taken at face
value'. Following D. C. Muecke here (see 'Further Reading') we might
classify this particular ironic sub-manœuvre as 'pretended advice'.
Clough's strategy in this poem has much in common with that of Swift
in his *An Argument against Abolishing Christianity*. Both authors advocate the right thing for the wrong reasons, as when Swift concludes
his tract by urging his readers not to abolish Christianity as the State
religion because this would upset Britain's allies, disrupt overseas in-
vestment, and so cause stocks and shares to fall 'at least one *percent*'.

Those of Clough's couplets which deviate from the 'because' pattern established in the first seem to rely more on ironic word-play than the others. 'Honour', for example, in the Fifth Commandment, is to be read as 'flatter'. What other examples of ironic word-play can be detected in the poem?

What values is Clough attacking? What are his own values? Write an essay in answer to these two questions, describing the ironic manœuvres employed by Clough and their intended effect upon the reader.

Exercise 4

As I suggested earlier, it is not always easy to recognize when an author is employing ironic manœuvres in a passage of writing. This is particularly the case when an author uses the device of first-person narration. In this exercise and the next, the reader is invited to decide whether the passages reproduced are intentionally ironic, unintentionally ironic, perhaps a mixture of both, not ironic at all, or insolubly ambiguous.

Decisions of this kind become extremely important in criticism of an evaluative kind. If we decide that a novel or a poem is insolubly ambiguous, which is perhaps to say that we cannot tell what its author meant by it, is it therefore a 'bad' piece of literature? Might we then want to try to distinguish between works which are *intentionally* ambiguous and those which are ambiguous because of the author's lack of control over his material? Does intention matter here? And how can we tell whether ambiguity is intentional or not?

Defoe's *Moll Flanders* is a novel which raises exactly these issues. Is it a first-rate piece of literature in its own right, or is it a ramshackle affair whose importance is mainly historical? Critics who think it first-rate, like Dorothy Van Ghent in *The English Novel: Form and Function*, argue that Defoe is an entirely conscious and thoroughly consistent ironist. Other highly reputable critics, such as Ian Watt in *The Rise of the Novel*, argue that '... it is surely certain that there is no consistently ironical attitude present in *Moll Flanders*'.

Defoe's other novels present similar difficulties of interpretation and evaluation. One can never be quite sure whether the pious remarks of his highwaymen and whores signal the presence of 'ironic impersonation', or whether they are inserted merely to give the reader a face-saving excuse for vicariously enjoying their thoroughly immoral antics.

In the following extract, for example, Roxana's respectable and unsuspecting Quaker husband is on the verge of accidentally finding out about her previous 'vile and vicious Life of Whoredom and Adultery', thanks to the Captain's innocent gossiping. Terrified out of her wits, Roxana contrives an 'accident' so that she can unburden herself to Amy, her servant and confidante. What reasons, if any, can be found for arguing that the extract is the work of a conscious and deliberate ironist?

> ... Now, in a word, the clouds began to thicken about me, and I had alarms on every side: my husband told me what the Captain had said; but very happily took it, that the Captain had brought a tale by halves, and having heard it one way, had told it another; and that neither could he understand the Captain, neither did the Captain understand himself; so he contented himself to tell me, he said, word for word, as the Captain delivered it.
>
> How I kept my husband from discovering my disorder, you shall hear presently; but let it suffice to say just now, that if my husband did not understand the Captain, nor the Captain understand himself, yet I understood them both very well; and to tell the truth, it was a worse shock than ever I had yet: invention supplied me indeed, with a sudden motion to avoid showing my surprise; for as my spouse and I was sitting by a little table, near the fire, I reached out my hand, as if I intended to take a spoon which lay on the other side, and threw one of the candles off of the table; and then snatching it up, started up upon my feet, and stooped to the lap of my gown, and took it in my hand; Oh! says I, my gown's spoiled; the candle has greased it prodigiously: this furnished me with an excuse to my spouse, to break off the discourse for the present, and call Amy down; and Amy not coming presently, I said to him, My dear, I must run upstairs, and put it off, and let Amy clean it a little; so my husband rose up too, and went into a closet, where he kept his papers and books, and fetched a book out, and sat down by himself, to read.
>
> Glad I was that I had got away; and up I run to Amy, who, as it happened, was alone; Oh Amy! says I, we are all utterly undone; and with that, I burst out a-crying, and could not speak a word for a great while.
>
> I cannot help saying, that some very good reflections offered themselves upon this head; it presently occurred, what a glorious testimony it is to the justice of Providence, and to the concern Providence has in guiding all the affairs of men, (even the least, as well as the greatest) that the most secret crimes are, by the most unforeseen accidents, brought to light, and discovered.
>
> Daniel Defoe: from *Roxana: The Fortunate Mistress*

Exercise 5

Ulysses

It little profits that an idle king,
By this still hearth, among these barren crags,
Matched with an agèd wife, I mete and dole
Unequal laws unto a savage race,
That hoard, and sleep, and feed, and know not me.
I cannot rest from travel; I will drink
Life to the lees. All times I have enjoyed

Greatly, have suffered greatly, both with those
That loved me, and alone; on shore, and when
Through scudding drifts the rainy Hyades
Vext the dim sea. I am become a name;
For always roaming with a hungry heart
Much have I seen and known; cities of men
And manners, climates, councils, governments,
Myself not least, but honoured of them all;
And drunk delight of battle with my peers,
Far on the ringing plains of windy Troy.
I am a part of all that I have met;
Yet all experience is an arch wherethro'
Gleams that untravelled world, whose margin fades
For ever and for ever when I move.
How dull it is to pause, to make an end,
To rust unburnished, not to shine in use!
As though to breathe were life! Life piled on life
Were all too little, and of one to me
Little remains; but every hour is saved
From that eternal silence, something more,
A bringer of new things; and vile it were
For some three suns to store and hoard myself,
And this gray spirit yearning in desire
To follow knowledge like a sinking star,
Beyond the utmost bound of human thought.

This is my son, mine own Telemachus,
To whom I leave the sceptre and the isle—
Well-loved of me, discerning to fulfil
This labour, by slow prudence to make mild
A rugged people, and through soft degrees
Subdue them to the useful and the good.
Most blameless is he, centred in the sphere
Of common duties, decent not to fail
In offices of tenderness, and pay
Meet adoration to my household gods,
When I am gone. He works his work, I mine.

There lies the port; the vessel puffs her sail:
There gloom the dark, broad seas. My mariners,
Souls that have toiled, and wrought, and thought with me—
That ever with a frolic welcome took
The thunder and the sunshine, and opposed
Free hearts, free foreheads—you and I are old;
Old age hath yet his honour and his toil.
Death closes all; but something ere the end,
Some work of noble note, may yet be done,
Not unbecoming men that strove with Gods.
The lights begin to twinkle from the rocks;

The long day wanes; the slow moon climbs; the deep
Moans round with many voices. Come, my friends,
'Tis not too late to seek a newer world.
Push off, and sitting well in order smite
The sounding furrows; for my purpose holds
To sail beyond the sunset, and the baths
Of all the western stars, until I die.

It may be that the gulfs will wash us down;
It may be we shall touch the Happy Isles,
And see the great Achilles, whom we knew.
Though much is taken, much abides; and though
We are not now that strength which in old days
Moved earth and heaven, that which we are, we are;
One equal temper of heroic hearts,
Made weak by time and fate, but strong in will
To strive, to seek, to find, and not to yield.

Alfred, Lord Tennyson

Tennyson's famous poem is of course a dramatic monologue. Does Tennyson wish us to approve of Ulysses as the epitome of heroic endeavour? Or does he wish us to disapprove of him as the epitome of selfishly romantic escapism: vainglorious, contemptuous of his wife and son, eager to shirk the routine responsibilities of ruling his people, and willing to sacrifice the lives of his old comrades to his own restless pursuit of novelty?

5
Tone

The overall tone of a piece of writing and any variations of tone which occur within it are highly important aspects which we should be able to recognize, and, if necessary draw attention to and comment upon. 'Tone' as a concept is not all that difficult to define. However, the particular aspect of a piece of writing which the term refers to is one which inexperienced readers of literature usually have great difficulty in registering accurately, and which experienced readers find considerable difficulty in talking about as accurately as they would wish.

The first point to be made about 'tone' is that when we talk about the tone 'of a passage' we are really talking about the tone of its *author* (as turned out to be the case with 'diction'). The second point to be made is that 'tone' is not a thing, but a concept. As a concept it refers to that aspect of an author's manner of writing which indicates the *kind* of response which he wishes or intends the reader to have. Writers indicate the kind of response they are after by providing a series of cues or signals, and we need to be able to detect these and to respond to them.

The analogy with 'tone of voice' in everyday spoken language is one which is usually made in discussions of tone in literature, and it is one which is worth pursuing here because it illuminates real problems which most of us encounter when reading literature.

The term is taken by analogy, then, from the term 'tone of voice', which is of course usually employed in describing human speech, not written language. When we talk about a speaker's 'tone of voice' we are in fact referring to all those highly subtle modulations and inflexions of stress and pitch and speed of delivery which tell a listener how the speaker would like him to respond; or, we might say, which tell him what particular category of response is being sought.

The same sentence, or even the same word, can be spoken in countless different tones of voice. For example, a friend might say to me: 'I hear that you crashed your car into a tree again last night.' His tone might be concerned, horrified, sarcastic, resigned, gleeful, or carefully neutral. Even an apparently critical remark such as 'He is always late for every appointment' can be said bitterly or, at the opposite extreme, playfully.

Most of us have learned through experience how to respond to these subtle cues in everyday conversation. We do occasionally misinterpret a speaker's tone, however, and begin to laugh (to our embarrassment) when he is in deadly earnest; or, if he adopts the dead-pan delivery of the ironist, we may respond earnestly when he intends us to laugh at what he is saying.

The dangers of misinterpreting tone are very much greater in the case of literature, where spoken inflexions (together with gestures and facial expressions) are replaced by nuances of written expression. Irony is particularly likely to be overlooked or misinterpreted, and it is worthwhile pointing out here that the concept of tone and the concept of irony overlap each other to a considerable extent. To misinterpret an author's tone is to mistake his intention, and in the end, in literature as in everyday conversation, the accurate registration of tone can only be the product of extensive experience.

Here, by way of example, is a short poem by Ben Jonson whose tone and intention could easily be mistaken by a too-serious reader:

Song: That Women are but Men's Shadows

Follow a shadow, it still flies you;
   Seem to fly it, it will pursue:
So court a mistress, she denies you;
   Let her alone, she will court you.
Say, are not women truly, then,
   Styled but the shadows of us men?
At morn, and even, shades are longest;
   At noon, they are or* short, or none:
So men at weakest, they are strongest,
   But grant us perfect,† they're not known.
Say, are not women truly, then,
   Styled but the shadows of us men?

Women, says Jonson, have been described as being only men's shadows; that is, they have no solid and independent personalities of their own, but depend upon men for their very existence. He then sets out to prove the truth of this by using two examples: women are like shadows in that you can never catch them, though they will follow you if you try to run away from them; also, they loom larger for a man in his infancy (morn) and old age (even), virtually disappearing when he is completely independent and mature (noon).

It would, of course, be a mistake to take this too seriously and to

* either
† fully-grown

complain of sexual discrimination. Jonson is not writing a male-chauvinist polemic, but directing our attention to his skill in developing an ingenious argument in verse which is both highly-wrought and deceptively simple. The poem is primarily an elegant *performance*, in short, and Jonson's tone is witty, playful, and good-humoured. To take this poem seriously would certainly be to mistake its author's intention.

There is an almost endless number of adjectives which might be used to describe tone in literature. An author's tone might be earnest, witty, mordant, whimsical, hesitant, serious, genial, sarcastic, playful, sardonic, hysterical, condescending, philosophical, elevated, frivolous, salacious, savage, light-hearted, arch, assertive, cynical, good-natured, dogmatic, maudlin, good-humoured, and so on. In a work of this size it is clearly impossible to provide examples of these and the many other possible varieties of tone.

Nor is it necessary, fortunately, for the distinctions mentioned are comparatively fine ones, and most students in practice need to be encouraged to distinguish between the far broader categories of writing whose tone is serious, and writing whose tone is serio-comic.

It needs to be said here that a great deal of so-called 'serious' literature is much more humorous, witty, and even light-hearted than many students appear to imagine. In Chapter 4 ('Irony') I stated that 'comedies, while clearly less grim than tragedies, are not less moral in their intentions'. In other words, literature can be 'serious' without being solemn, and it can be 'comic' without being merely frivolous. It can in fact be, and very often is, 'serio-comic': both serious and comic at the same time. There are of course a great many works of literature whose tone is that of a sustained high seriousness, such as Yeats's poem 'Leda and the Swan' or Matthew Arnold's 'Dover Beach'. But there is at least an equal number, ranging from Shakespeare's *Twelfth Night* to Joyce's *Ulysses*, whose tone is best described as 'serio-comic'. Rather than multiply examples here, I refer the reader to my comments on particular passages in Chapters 4, 7, and 8. Looked at from the point of view of their tone, these examples are probably enough to establish that such major authors as Jane Austen, Charles Dickens, John Dryden, George Eliot, William Faulkner, Henry Fielding, James Joyce, Alexander Pope and Oscar Wilde can all be serious in their moral intentions, whilst writing in a humorous manner.

All of these writers are critical of human failings, of course, and even satirical, and this is a matter which presents problems for many readers, who find it difficult to distinguish between the kinds of criticism intended. The *kind* of criticism intended is indicated by the tone, and the most important thing to remember here is that there are many kinds and levels of criticism and many kinds and levels of satire, just as there are many kinds and levels of irony. Critical comments of any kind can be quite unalike in their tone: as we saw earlier they can be bitter at one extreme, and playful at the other, with many possible shades in between. The same is true of both parody and satire. Max Beerbohm's delightful collection of parodies *A Christmas Garland*, for example, contains a parody (ironic impersonation) of Henry James's writing which though critical is affectionate and even admiring in tone, together with a parody of Kipling's writing whose tone is hostile and contemptuous. Satires such as Pope's can be genial and light-hearted in tone ('The Rape of the Lock'), or destructive and dismissive (*The Dunciad*).

For a student wishing to describe the tone of a particular passage of satirical writing, two useful adjectives are available: 'Horatian', and 'Juvenalian'. These words derive from the names of two of the greatest Roman satirists: Horace and Juvenal respectively. The tone of Horatian satire is amused and tolerant, while that of Juvenalian satire is aggressive and contemptuous. The distinction between the two types of satire is no more than a rough-and-ready one, of course, and many satires have a mixed tone. Such are the satires of Evelyn Waugh, in which, as A. E. Dyson admirably puts it: 'Satiric ruthlessness is tempered ... with bitter-sweet nostalgia for the scenes and people satirised.' Nevertheless, it seems reasonable to describe the tone of George Eliot's satirical description of Mr. Casaubon as 'Horatian', and the tone of the following description of the effeminate Lord Hervey, from Pope's 'Epistle to Dr. Arbuthnot', as 'Juvenalian':

> Yet let me flap this bug with gilded wings,
> This painted child of dirt, that stinks and stings;
>
> *   *   *
>
> Eternal smiles his emptiness betray,
> As shallow streams run dimpling all the way.
> Whether in florid impotence he speaks,
> And, as the prompter breathes, the puppet squeaks;
> Or at the ear of *Eve*, familiar Toad,
> Half froth, half venom, spits himself abroad,
> In puns, or politics, or tales, or lies,
> Or spite, or smut, or rhymes, or blasphemies.
> His wit all seesaw, between *that* and *this*,
> Now high, now low, now master up, now miss,
> And he himself one vile Antithesis.

The most difficult kind of tone to gauge accurately is probably that of 'black humour', or 'black comedy'. In this, the author invites us to respond in two ways simultaneously: to wince at the macabre and grotesque elements in human life, and at the same time to appreciate their comic aspects. Corpses find particular favour with black humorists. Here, by way of example, is Ford Madox Ford's description of the discovery of the body of the victim of a heart-attack in his novel *The Good Soldier*:

> She had not cared to look round Maisie's rooms at first. Now, as soon as she came in, she perceived, sticking out beyond the bed, a small pair of feet in high-heeled shoes. Maisie had died in the effort to strap up a great portmanteau. She had died so grotesquely that her little body had fallen forward into the trunk, and it had closed upon her, like the jaws of a gigantic alligator. The key was in her hand. Her dark hair, like the hair of a Japanese, had come down and covered her body and face.
>
> Leonora lifted her up—she was the merest feather-weight—and laid her on the bed with her hair about her. She was smiling, as if she had just scored a goal in a hockey match.

We would be mistaking the tone here if we were merely appalled, as we would in the following extract from William Faulkner's *As I Lay Dying*. This describes the entry of the Bundren family into the town of Mottson, as they carry their mother's putrefying corpse in a wagon to be buried in Jefferson, Missouri:

> It was Albert told me about the rest of it. He said the wagon was stopped in front of Grummet's hardware store, with the ladies all scattering up and down the street with handkerchiefs to their noses, and a crowd of hard-nosed men and boys standing round the wagon, listening to the marshal arguing with the man. ... It had been dead eight days, Albert said. ... It must have been like a piece of rotten cheese coming into an ant-hill, in that ramshackle wagon that Albert said folks were scared would fall all to pieces before they could get it out of town, with that home-made box and another fellow with a broken leg lying on a quilt on top of it, and the father and a little boy sitting on the seat and the marshal trying to make them get out of town. ...
>
> They had stopped to buy some cement. The other son was in Grummet's, trying to make Grummet break a sack and let him have ten cent's worth, and finally Grummet broke the sack to get him out. They wanted the cement to fix the fellow's broken leg, someway.
>
> 'Why, you'll kill him,' the marshal said. 'You'll cause him to lose his leg. You take him on to a doctor, and you get this thing buried as soon as you can. Don't you know that you're liable to jail for endangering the public health?'
>
> 'We're doing the best we can,' the father said.

A mother's decaying body, a son's broken leg, the meanness of the other members of the family who wish to set that leg in cement rather than pay a doctor, and who even haggle about the price of the cement: these things are potentially appalling. Yet the scene is described as if it were farcical. It would be interesting to re-write this scene, changing its tone in such a way that the incident became wholly appalling and/or pathetic, and the reader is invited to try the experiment of doing so.

There is a strong tradition of 'black comedy' in Western European drama which runs from Euripides (e.g. *Hippolytus*) down to Ibsen (e.g. *The Wild Duck*) and the plays of Beckett and Ionesco. Shakespeare's *Measure for Measure* is in this tradition, as are the plays of such Jacobean dramatists as Webster and Tourneur and such contemporary English dramatists as Harold Pinter and Joe Orton (e.g. *Loot*). Many of the poems and novels of Thomas Hardy have a blackly humorous tone (e.g. *Jude the Obscure*), and the same vein has been exploited in the short story by 'Saki' (H. H. Munro) and in poetry by William Plomer (in such satirical ballads as 'The Flying Bum').

Against the difficulties in the way of our registering this particular tone accurately, we may set the fact that it has become more widespread during recent years in such novels as Joseph Heller's *Catch-22*, such films as *M*A*S*H*, and such television serials as *Till Death Us Do Part*.

In conclusion, it should be emphasized that an author's tone is most definitely not a separable element which is 'in' a passage of literary writing.

Rather, it is something which has to be inferred *from* the passage as a whole. We need to be able to say what an author's tone is, and then if necessary to specify what it depends on: such as the author's diction, figurative language, narrative point of view, ironical manœuvres, and his use of 'pattern'.

This last major concept to be dealt with singly will be discussed in the chapter which follows.

Exercises

Questions and comments on the five passages which follow are fewer than have been thought necessary hitherto, and the prose extracts are somewhat longer. The reader is invited to give a brief description of the tone of each passage, supporting his conclusions by detailed reference to the text, and employing as much as possible of what he has learned in previous chapters about diction, figurative language, narrative point of view, etc.

Before embarking on the passages below, the reader might well re-read some of those used in earlier exercises and consider what might be said about their tone. Particularly interesting in this respect are: Kipling: 'The Bridegroom' (p. 14); Dickens: from *Martin Chuzzle-wit* (p. 25); Thackeray: from *Vanity Fair* (p. 28); Fielding: from *Joseph Andrews* (p. 37); Hardy: 'The Ruined Maid' (p. 63).

Exercise 1

[The Village Schoolmaster]

Beside yon straggling fence that skirts the way,
With blossomed furze unprofitably gay,
There, in his noisy mansion, skilled to rule,
The village master taught his little school;
A man severe he was, and stern to view,
I knew him well, and every truant knew;
Well had the boding tremblers learned to trace
The day's disasters in his morning face;
Full well they laughed with counterfeited glee,
At all his jokes, for many a joke had he;
Full well the busy whisper circling round,
Conveyed the dismal tidings when he frowned;
Yet he was kind, or if severe in aught,
The love he bore to learning was in fault;
The village all declared how much he knew;
'Twas certain he could write, and cipher too;
Lands he could measure, terms and tides presage,
And even the story ran that he could gauge.
In arguing too, the parson owned his skill,
For even though vanquished, he could argue still;
While words of learned length, and thundering sound,
Amazed the gazing rustics ranged around;
And still they gazed, and still the wonder grew,
That one small head could carry all he knew.
But past is all his fame. The very spot
Where many a time he triumphed, is forgot.
Near yonder thorn, that lifts its head on high,
Where once the signpost caught the passing eye,
Low lies that house where nut-brown draughts inspired,
Where graybeard Mirth and smiling Toil retired,
Where village statesmen talked with looks profound,
And news much older than their ale went round.
Oliver Goldsmith: from 'The Deserted Village'.

'Fault' was pronounced 'fought'; 'tides' as in 'Eastertide' and 'Whit-suntide'; 'gauge': 'calculate fluid measure'; 'owned': 'admitted'.
Could Goldsmith's tone fairly be described as 'patronizing' here?

Exercise 2

[Mrs. Gamp]

'A little dull, but not so bad as might be,' Mrs. Gamp remarked. 'I'm glad to see a parapidge, in case of fire, and lots of roofs and chimley-pots to walk upon.'
It will be seen from these remarks that Mrs. Gamp was looking out of a window. When she had exhausted the prospect, she tried the easy-chair, which she indignantly declared was 'harder than a brickbadge.' Next she pursued her researches among the physic-bottles, glasses, jugs, and tea-cups; and when she had entirely satisfied her curiosity on all these subjects of investigation, she untied her bonnet-strings and strolled up to the bedside to take a look at the patient.

A young man—dark and not ill-looking—with long black hair, that seemed the blacker for the whiteness of the bedclothes. His eyes were partly open, and he never ceased to roll his head from side to side upon the pillow, keeping his body almost quiet. He did not utter words; but every now and then gave vent to an expression of impatience or fatigue, sometimes of surprise; and still his restless head—oh, weary, weary hour!—went to and fro without a moment's intermission.

Mrs. Gamp solaced herself with a pinch of snuff, and stood looking at him with her head inclined a little sideways, as a connoisseur might gaze upon a doubtful work of art. By degrees, a horrible remembrance of one branch of her calling took possession of the woman; and stooping down, she pinned his wandering arms against his sides, to see how he would look if laid out as a dead man. Hideous as it may appear, her fingers itched to compose his limbs in that last marble attitude.

'Ah!' said Mrs. Gamp, walking away from the bed, 'he'd make a lovely corpse.'

She now proceeded to unpack her bundle; lighted a candle with the aid of a fire-box on the drawers; filled a small kettle, as a preliminary to refreshing herself with a cup of tea in the course of the night; laid what she called 'a little bit of fire,' for the same philanthropic purpose, and also set forth a small teaboard, that nothing might be wanting for her comfortable enjoyment. These preparations occupied so long, that when they were brought to a conclusion it was high time to think about supper; so she rang the bell and ordered it.

'I think, young woman,' said Mrs. Gamp to the assistant chambermaid, in a tone of expressive weakness, 'that I could pick a little bit of pickled salmon, with a nice little sprig of fennel, and a sprinkling of white pepper. I takes new bread, my dear, with jest a little pat of fresh butter, and a mossel of cheese. In case there should be such a thing as a cowcumber in the 'ouse, will you be so kind as to bring it, for I'm rather partial to 'em, and they does a world of good in a sick room. If they draws the Brighton Old Tipper here, I takes *that* ale at night, my love; it bein' considered wakeful by the doctors. And whatever you do, young woman, don't bring more than a shilling's-worth of gin and water-warm when I rings the bell a second time, for that is always my allowance, and I never takes a drop beyond!'

Having preferred these moderate requests, Mrs. Gamp observed that she would stand at the door until the order was executed, to the end that the patient might not be disturbed by her opening it a second time; and therefore she would thank the young woman to 'look sharp.'

A tray was brought with everything upon it, even to the cucumber; and Mrs. Gamp accordingly sat down to eat and drink in high good humour. The extent to which she availed herself of the vinegar, and supped up that refreshing fluid with the blade of her knife, can scarcely be expressed in narrative.

'Ah!' sighed Mrs. Gamp, as she meditated over the warm shilling's-worth, 'what a blessed thing it is—living in a wale—to be contented! What a blessed thing it is to make sick people happy in their beds, and never mind one's self as long as one can do a service! I don't believe a finer cowcumber was ever grow'd. I'm sure I never seen one!'

She moralised in the same vein until her glass was empty, and then administered the patient's medicine, by the simple process of clutching his windpipe, to make him gasp, and immediately pouring it down his throat.

'I a'most forgot the piller, I declare!' said Mrs. Gamp, drawing it away. 'There! Now he's comfortable as can be, *I*'m sure! I must try to make myself as much so as I can.'

With this view, she went about the construction of an extemporaneous bed in the easy-chair, with the addition of the next easy one for her feet.

Charles Dickens: from *Martin Chuzzlewit*

'Wale': Mrs. Gamp's pronunciation of 'vale'. She has earlier referred to life as 'this Piljian's Projiss of a mortal wale': meaning The Valley of the Shadow of Death in Bunyan's *Pilgrim's Progress*.

In the preface to the 1849 edition of *Martin Chuzzlewit*, Dickens wrote as follows: '... I hope I have taken every opportunity of showing the want of sanitary improvements in the neglected dwellings of the poor. Mrs. Sarah Gamp is a representation of the hired attendant on the poor in sickness'.

Does Dickens's tone in the above extract invite the reader's indignation at Mrs. Gamp's shortcomings as a professional sick-nurse?

Exercise 3

The Contretemps

A forward rush by the lamp in the gloom,
    And we clasped, and almost kissed;
  . But she was not the woman whom
    I had promised to meet in the thawing brume
On that harbour-bridge; nor was I he of her tryst.

So loosening from me swift she said:
    'O why, why feign to be
The one I had meant!—to whom I have sped
To fly with, being so sorrily wed!'
—'Twas thus and thus that she upbraided me.

My assignation had struck upon
    Some others' like it, I found.
And her lover rose on the night anon;
    And then her husband entered on
The lamplit, snowflaked, sloppiness around.

'Take her and welcome, man!' he cried:
   'I wash my hands of her.
I'll find me twice as good a bride!'
   —All this to me, whom he had eyed,
Plainly, as his wife's planned deliverer.

And next the lover: 'Little I knew,
   Madam, you had a third!
Kissing here in my very view!'
   —Husband and lover then withdrew.
I let them; and I told them not they erred.

Why not? Well, there faced she and I—
   Two strangers who'd kissed, or near,
Chancewise. To see stand weeping by
   A woman once embraced, will try
The tension of a man the most austere.

So it began; and I was young,
   She pretty, by the lamp,
As flakes came waltzing down among
   The waves of her clinging hair, that hung
Heavily on her temples, dark and damp.

And there alone still stood we two;
   She one cast off for me,
Or so it seemed; while night ondrew,
   Forcing a parley what should do
We twain hearts caught in one catastrophe.

In stranded souls a common strait
   Wakes latencies unknown,
Whose impulse may precipitate
   A life-long leap. The hour was late,
And there was the Jersey boat with its funnel agroan.

'Is wary walking worth much pother?'
   It grunted, as still it stayed.
'One pairing is as good as another
   Where all is venture! Take each other,
And scrap the oaths that you have aforetime made.'

—Of the four involved there walks but one
   On earth at this late day.
And what of the chapter so begun?
   In that odd complex what was done?
Well; happiness comes in full to none:
Let peace lie on lulled lips: I will not say.
Thomas Hardy

How would you describe the tone of Hardy's dramatic monologue?
Write a short paragraph describing the tone of the poem, and then

support your conclusions by a full and detailed interpretation of the text.

Exercise 4

[Becky and Amelia]

[Becky has left England because of a scandal and is leading a bohemian life in a German spa-town. Accidentally rediscovered by her old school-friend Amelia, she tells her a sob-story about her misfortunes. Becky is completely indifferent to her own son 'little Rawdon', whilst Amelia is maternally obsessed with her son 'Georgy'.]

Frankness and kindness like Amelia's were likely to touch even such a hardened little reprobate as Becky. She returned Emmy's caresses and kind speeches with something very like gratitude, and an emotion which, if it was not lasting, for a moment was almost genuine. That was a lucky stroke of hers about the child 'torn from her arms shrieking'. It was by that harrowing misfortune that Becky had won her friend back, and it was one of the very first points, we may be certain, upon which our poor simple little Emmy began to talk to her new-found acquaintance.

'And so they took your darling child from you?' our simpleton cried out. 'O Rebecca, my poor dear suffering friend, I know what it is to lose a boy, and to feel for those who have lost one. But please Heaven yours will be restored to you, as a merciful merciful Providence has brought me back mine.'

'The child, my child? Oh, yes, my agonies were frightful,' Becky owned, not perhaps without a twinge of conscience. It jarred upon her, to be obliged to commence instantly to tell lies in reply to so much confidence and simplicity. But that is the misfortune of beginning with this kind of forgery. When one fib becomes due as it were, you must forge another to take up the old acceptance; and so the stock of your lies in circulation inevitably multiplies, and the danger of detection increases every day.

'My agonies,' Becky continued, 'were terrible (I hope she won't sit down on the bottle) when they took him away from me; I thought I should die; but I fortunately had a brain fever, during which my doctor gave me up, and—and I recovered, and—and here I am, poor and friendless.'

'How old is he?' Emmy asked.

'Eleven,' said Becky.

'Eleven!' cried the other. 'Why, he was born the same year with Georgy, who is'——

'I know, I know,' Becky cried out, who had in fact quite forgotten all about little Rawdon's age. 'Grief has made me forget so many things, dearest Amelia. I am very much changed: half wild sometimes. He was eleven when they took him away from me. Bless his sweet face; I have never seen it again.'

'Was he fair or dark?' went on the absurd little Emmy. 'Show me his hair.'

Becky almost laughed at her simplicity. 'Not to-day, love,—some other time, when my trunks arrive from Leipsic, whence I came to this place,—and a little drawing of him, which I made in happy days.'

'Poor Becky, poor Becky!' said Emmy. 'How thankful, how thankful I ought to be;' (though I doubt whether that practice of piety inculcated upon us by our womankind in early youth, namely, to be thankful because we are better off than somebody else, be a very rational religious exercise;) and then she began to think, as usual, how her son was the handsomest, the best, and the cleverest boy in the whole world.

'You will see my Georgy,' was the best thing Emmy could think of to console Becky. If anything could make her comfortable, that would.

And so the two women continued talking for an hour or more, during which Becky had the opportunity of giving her new friend a full and complete version of her private history.

W. M. Thackeray: from *Vanity Fair*

'The bottle': the brandy-bottle which Becky had hidden in the bed when an earlier visitor arrived, together with a rouge-pot and a plate of cold meat.

Thackeray describes Amelia as a 'simpleton'. Does he mean this ironically, as Fielding does in *Jonathan Wild* when he describes the virtuous Heartfree as 'possessed of several great weaknesses of mind'? Are we to approve of Amelia's frankness and kindness to the 'hardened little reprobate'? Or are we being invited to side with Becky in the face of her gullibility? Or is Thackeray's depiction of both characters intentionally ambiguous? What are some possible meanings of the word 'simple'?

(Readers interested in the question of intentional and unintentional ambiguity might like to read *Vanity Fair* and compare it with *Moll Flanders*. Perhaps by 'intentional' ambiguity we mean 'demonstrably systematic' ambiguity?).

Exercise 5

Tone is not necessarily uniform throughout a work of literature. It is more likely to modulate from stanza to stanza, scene to scene, and chapter to chapter. The particularly long extract which follows has been included to emphasize this important point.

Dr. Aziz and his friends are, of course, Moslems in the British India of the 1920s. Rafi is hinting that Dr. Aziz and Professor Godbole have been poisoned by Fielding, the Englishman who is Principal of the local Government College.

... Someone had called to inquire. The thought of sympathy increased his fever, and with a sincere groan he wrapped himself in his quilt.

'Aziz, my dear fellow, we are greatly concerned,' said Hamidullah's voice. One, two, three, four bumps, as people sat down upon his bed.

'When a doctor falls ill it is a serious matter,' said the voice of Mr. Syed Mohammed, the assistant engineer.

'When an engineer falls ill, it is equally important,' said the voice of Mr. Haq, a police inspector.

'Oh, yes, we are all jolly important, our salaries prove it.'

'Dr. Aziz took tea with our Principal last Thursday afternoon,' piped Rafi, the engineer's nephew. 'Professor Godbole, who also attended, has sickened too, which seems rather a curious thing, sir, does it not?'

Flames of suspicion leapt up in the breast of each man. 'Humbug!' exclaimed Hamidullah, in authoritative tones, quenching them.

'Humbug, most certainly,' echoed the others, ashamed of themselves. The wicked schoolboy, having failed to start a scandal, lost confidence and stood up with his back to the wall.

'Is Professor Godbole ill?' inquired Aziz, penetrated by the news. 'I am sincerely sorry.' Intelligent and compassionate, his face peeped out of the bright crimson folds of the quilt. 'How do you do, Mr. Syed Mohammed, Mr. Haq? How very kind of you to inquire after my health! How do you do, Hamidullah? But you bring me bad news. What is wrong with him, the excellent fellow?'

'Why don't you answer, Rafi? You're the great authority,' said his uncle.

'Yes, Rafi's the great man,' said Hamidullah, rubbing it in. 'Rafi is the Sherlock Holmes of Chandrapore. Speak up, Rafi.'

Less than the dust, the schoolboy murmured the word 'Diarrhoea', but took courage as soon as it had been uttered, for it improved his position. Flames of suspicion shot up again in the breasts of his elders, though in a different direction. Could what was called diarrhoea really be an early case of cholera?

'If this is so, this is a very serious thing: this is scarcely the end of March. Why have I not been informed? cried Aziz.

'Dr. Panna Lal attends him, sir.'

'Oh yes, both Hindus; there we have it; they hang together like flies and keep everything dark. Rafi, come here. Sit down. Tell me all the details. Is there vomiting also?'

'Oh yes indeed, sir, and the serious pains.'

'That settles it. In twenty-four hours he will be dead.'

Everybody looked and felt shocked, but Professor Godbole had diminished his appeal by linking himself with a co-religionist. He moved them less than when he had appeared as a suffering individual. Before long they began to condemn him as a source of infection. 'All illness proceeds from Hindus,' Mr. Haq said. Mr. Syed Mohammed had visited religious fairs, at Allahabad, at Ujjain, and described them with biting scorn. At Allahabad there was flowing water, which carried impurities away, but at Ujjain the little river Sipra was banked up, and thousands of bathers deposited their germs in the pool. He spoke with disgust of the hot sun, the cowdung and marigold flowers, and the encampment of saddhus, some of whom strode stark naked through the streets. Asked what was the name of the chief idol at Ujjain, he replied that he did not know, he had disdained to inquire, he really could not waste his time over such trivialities. His outburst took some time, and in his excitement he fell into Punjabi (he came from that side) and was unintelligible.

Aziz liked to hear his religion praised. It soothed the surface of his mind, and allowed beautiful images to form beneath. When the engineer's noisy tirade was finished, he said, 'That is exactly my own view.' He held up his hand, palm outward, his eyes began to glow, his heart to fill with tenderness. Issuing still farther from his quilt, he recited a poem by Ghalib. It had no connexion with anything that had gone before, but it came from his heart and spoke to theirs. They were overwhelmed by its pathos; pathos, they agreed, is the highest quality in art; a poem should touch the hearer with a sense of his own weakness, and should institute some comparison between mankind and flowers. The squalid bedroom grew quiet; the silly intrigues, the gossip, the shallow discontent were stilled, while words accepted as immortal filled the indifferent air. Not as a call to battle, but as a calm assurance came the feeling that India was one: Moslem: always had been: an assurance that lasted until they looked out of the door. Whatever Ghalib had felt, he had anyhow lived in India, and this consolidated it for them: he had gone with his own tulips and roses, but tulips and roses do not go. And the sister kingdoms of the north—Arabia, Persia, Ferghana, Turkestan—stretched out their hands as he sang, sadly, because all beauty is sad, and greeted ridiculous Chandrapore, where every street and house was divided against itself, and told her that she was a continent and a unity.

Of the company, only Hamidullah had any comprehension of poetry. The minds of the others were inferior and rough. Yet they listened with pleasure, because literature had not been divorced from their civilization. The police inspector, for instance, did not feel that Aziz had degraded himself by reciting, nor break into the cheery guffaw with which an Englishman averts the infection of beauty. He just sat with his mind empty, and when his thoughts, which were mainly ignoble, flowed back into it they had a pleasant freshness. The poem had done no 'good' to anyone, but it was a passing reminder, a breath from the divine lips of beauty, a nightingale between two worlds of dust. Less explicit than the call to Krishna, it voiced our loneliness nevertheless, our isolation, our need for the Friend who never comes yet is not entirely disproved. Aziz it left thinking about women again, but in a different way: less definite, more intense. Sometimes poetry had this effect on him, sometimes it only increased his local desires, and he never knew beforehand which effect would ensue: he could discover no rule for this or for anything else in life.

Hamidullah had called in on his way to a worrying committee of notables, nationalist in tendency, where Hindus, Moslems, two Sikhs, two Parsis, a Jain, and a Native Christian tried to like one another more than came natural to them. As long as someone abused the English, all went well, but nothing constructive had been achieved, and if the English were to leave India, the committee would vanish also.

E. M. Forster: from *A Passage to India*

6
Pattern

The five chapters preceding have all dealt with terms and concepts commonly used in literary criticism, and in discussing them I have kept fairly close to established usage. 'Pattern' is a common enough word, and critics often talk about 'patterns' of different kinds in works of literature: patterns of syntax, or sentence-structure; patterns of 'imagery' (i.e. figurative language); and sound-patterns, especially in poetry.

However, I would like to use the term in my own extended sense to mean 'the degree of patterning' in a piece of literature, whether in prose or verse. Also, I wish to suggest that patterns of syntax are very much more important than the patterns of sound produced by such devices as alliteration, assonance, and (in verse) rhyme and metre. Patterns of sound often *re-inforce* patterns of syntax, and therefore of meaning, but are comparatively unimportant in themselves.

What we call 'a pattern' is something which is made up of the same kinds of unit, repeated in the same kinds of way. A pattern of syntax, then, is one in which the same grammatical kinds of word (such as nouns, verbs, and adjectives) are repeated in the same kinds of sequence. Let us look to begin with at two passages, one more patterned than the other:

> When my uncle Toby first mentioned the grenadier, my father, I said, fell down with his nose flat to the quilt, and as suddenly as if my uncle Toby had shot him; but it was not added that every other limb and member of my father instantly relapsed with his nose into the same precise attitude in which he lay first described; so that when corporal Trim left the room, and my father found himself disposed to rise off the bed—he had all the little preparatory movements to run over again, before he could do it. Attitudes are nothing, madam—'tis the transition from one attitude to another—like the preparation and resolution of the discord into harmony, which is all in all.

> Meantime the family forces were perpetually encountering each other in diverse parts of the neighbourhood; and, as no one branch of the Chuzzlewit tree had ever been known to agree with another within the memory of man, there was such a skirmishing, and flouting, and snapping off of heads, in the metaphorical sense of that expression; such a bandying of words and calling of names; such an upturning of noses and wrinkling of brows; such a formal interment of good feelings and violent resurrection of ancient grievances; as had never been known in those quiet parts since the earliest record of their civilised existence.

It should be clear that the second passage, which is from Dickens's *Martin Chuzzlewit*, is much more patterned than the first, which is from Sterne's *Tristram Shandy*. This example of Sterne's prose contains no kinds of words, such as nouns, verbs and adjectives, repeated in the same kinds of sequence. The passage from Dickens, on the other hand, is full of repetitions such as the following, which can be put one above the other to make the symmetrical patterning more obvious:

	present participle	+	*noun*	+	*present participle*	+	*noun*
such a	bandying	of	words	and	calling	of	names
such an	upturning	of	noses	and	wrinkling	of	brows

(i) Parallel and Antithesis in Prose and Verse

The device used by Dickens in the example just given is that of 'parallel', or the repetition of grammatically similar words of similar meaning ('bandying', 'calling'; 'upturning', 'wrinkling') in similar sequences. 'Parallel' and its variant 'antithesis' are the two most important patterns of syntax which we need to be aware of. Before 'antithesis' is discussed, here are two more examples of 'parallel' (or 'parallelism'), the first from John Lyly's *Euphues: The Anatomy of Wit* (1578) and the second from T. S. Eliot's *Four Quartets*. In both examples, the parallel syntax serves to emphasize *similarities* in meaning between the items presented:

> Doth not the rust fret the hardest iron if it be not used? Doth not the moth eat the finest garment if it be not worn? Doth not moss grow on the smoothest stone if it be not stirred? Doth not impiety infect the wisest wit if it be given to idleness? Is not the standing water sooner frozen than the running stream? Is not he that sitteth more subject to sleep than he that walketh?

> Keeping time,
> Keeping the rhythm in their dancing
> As in their living in the living seasons
> The time of the seasons and the constellations
> The time of milking and the time of harvest
> The time of the coupling of man and woman
> And that of beasts. Feet rising and falling.
> Eating and drinking. Dung and death.

'Antithesis' is the repetition of grammatically similar words of *opposed or contrary* meaning in similar sequences. Here, the parallel syntax serves to emphasize *contrast* in meaning, as in the two following examples from the preface to George Bernard Shaw's play *Heartbreak*

House. The first of these is also a good example of the minor part played by alliteration in re-inforcing antitheses:

> There was only one virtue, pugnacity: only one vice, pacifism.
> It rhapsodized about love; but it believed in cruelty.

Eighteenth-century poetry is full of such antitheses as the two following by Alexander Pope:

> Charms strike the sight, but merit wins the soul.
> Willing to wound, and yet afraid to strike.

Finally, the following magnificently elaborate sentence from Dr. Johnson's preface to his *Dictionary of the English Language* will help us to understand some of the effects which can be produced by patterns of syntax:

> When I took the first survey of my undertaking, I found our speech copious without order, and energetic without rules: wherever I turned my view, there was perplexity to be disentangled, and confusion to be regulated; choice was to be made out of boundless variety, without any established principle of selection; adulterations were to be detected, without a settled test of purity; and modes of expression to be rejected or received, without the suffrages of any writers of classical reputation or acknowledged authority.

Johnson's manner of writing could hardly be more different from that of Sterne, in the passage quoted earlier from *Tristram Shandy*. Where Johnson's syntax is formal and regular, Sterne's is colloquial and irregular.

The effects of this difference can be expressed, first of all, in terms of 'tone'. Johnson's tone is formal and elevated; its effect is to invite our most serious and respectful attention. Sterne's tone is informal and conversational; its effect is to invite the amused and relaxed attention normally paid to a teller of shaggy-dog stories. The terms 'formal' and 'colloquial', incidentally, are as useful for describing syntax as they are for describing diction (see Chapter 1).

Secondly, the effects of such differences in degree of patterning can also usefully be thought of in terms of 'distance' (see Chapter 3: 'Narrative Point of View'). The higher the degree of patterning, the more detached the author usually is from his subject-matter. The lower the degree of patterning, the more likely is the author to be involved in and sympathetic to his subject-matter. This is certainly the case when the passage quoted earlier from Dickens's *Martin Chuzzlewit* is also compared with the passage from *Tristram Shandy*: Dickens's patterns of syntax contribute to his unsympathetic presentation of the members of the Chuzzlewit family. This point about 'distance' can also be put in another way: the higher the degree of patterning, the more is the reader made aware of the pattern*er*. That is, the author increasingly draws attention to himself as creator and controller of what is being presented (to himself as 'performer', in other words. See the comment on Ben Jonson's 'That Women are but Men's Shadows' in Chapter 5: 'Tone', and note that poem's high degree of patterning).

The third and most important effect of a high degree of formal patterning, which is of course closely connected with the two effects already described, is to express a systematized view of reality itself: to imply that the bewildering variety of human life and human values can be reduced to an organized scheme of things. This is particularly the case with argumentative writing such as that of Pope and Johnson. Dr. Johnson himself gives us the clue to this effect, when he writes: '... there was perplexity to be disentangled, and confusion to be regulated ...' Symmetrical patterns of syntax have the effect of disentangling perplexity, and regulating confusion: they seek to persuade us that an orderly and logical view of the human condition is possible, and that the author's scheme of things is the correct one.

The way in which such patterns of syntax 'regulate confusion' is by emphasizing similarities on the one hand, and by emphasizing differences on the other. Parellels emphasize similarities, whilst antitheses emphasize differences, thus allowing aspects of the human condition to be presented in highly simplified, almost diagrammatic terms. In the most extreme cases, as in the polemical prose of George Bernard Shaw, antitheses invite the reader to think in completely dualistic or 'black-and-white' categories such as 'The Dumb Capables and the Noisy Incapables' or 'The Ephemeral Thrones and the Eternal Theatre' (chapter-headings from the preface to *Heartbreak House*).

A major effect of imposing such patterns of logical thought and syntax on human experience is of course to exclude and ignore anything which cannot be fitted into them. At the other extreme from Dr. Johnson and George Bernard Shaw are those authors, such as Sterne and D. H. Lawrence, who do not seek to impose any hard-and-fast pattern on reality, but try instead to reproduce the flux of life in what appears to them to be its general shapelessness (see the passage from Lawrence reproduced at the end of this chapter). However, before we pass on to a particular aspect of patterning in verse, it should be pointed out that the examples so far cited have been extreme cases of patterning or the lack of it. Most authors inhabit the middle ground between Sterne and Dr. Johnson; the latter does not always write in a highly patterned way, nor does D. H. Lawrence always write in a completely unpatterned way.

(ii) Pattern in Verse

There are many kinds of pattern which can be employed in verse: patterns of syntax and sound such as those already touched upon, and such traditional patterned forms as the pentameter line, the heroic couplet, the Spenserian stanza, the sonnet, and the limerick. This sub-section deals briefly with a general aspect of pattern in verse which is of basic importance whatever the traditional form being used, and hence constitutes a distinctive feature which we need to be aware of.

Whatever the traditional form being used, we should always be aware of the extent to which the structure of the author's sentences coincides or does not coincide with the structure of his lines of verse. To use the traditional terms: we should always notice whether the poet's lines are mostly 'run-on', or mostly 'end-stopped', or whether he uses as many of one kind as of the other.

In the following extract from Goldsmith's *The Deserted Village*, all the lines are end-stopped. Each ends with a punctuation-mark which indicates the conclusion of a phrase, clause, or sentence:

> Sweet Auburn, loveliest village of the plain,
> Where health and plenty cheered the labouring swain,
> Where smiling spring its earliest visit paid,
> And parting summer's lingering blooms delayed,
> Dear lovely bowers of innocence and ease,
> Seats of my youth, when every sport could please,
> How often have I loitered o'er the green,
> Where humble happiness endeared each scene.
> How often have I paused on every charm,
> The sheltered cot, the cultivated farm,
> The never failing brook, the busy mill,
> The decent church that topt the neighbouring hill,
> The hawthorn bush, with seats beneath the shade,
> For talking age and whispering lovers made!

In the following extract from Wordsworth's poem 'Michael', on the other hand, most of the lines are run-on. The sentences 'run on' from line to line, and most of the punctuation-marks occur in the middle of lines, rather than at their ends:

> While in this sort the simple household lived
> From day to day, to Michael's ear there came
> Distressful tidings. Long before the time
> Of which I speak, the Shepherd had been bound

> In surety for his brother's son, a man
> Of an industrious life, and ample means—
> But unforeseen misfortunes suddenly
> Had pressed upon him,—and old Michael now
> Was summoned to discharge the forfeiture,
> A grievous penalty, but little less
> Than half his substance. This unlooked-for claim
> At the first hearing, for a moment took
> More hope out of his life than he supposed
> That any old man ever could have lost.

Goldsmith's end-stopped lines emphasize the rhyming words and draw attention to the verse as verse, i.e. as a skilful performance. As in the prose extract by Dr. Johnson, we are made continuously aware of the author's directing and controlling presence, and what was said about tone, distance and the presentation of an orderly scheme of things in Dr. Johnson's prose could also be applied to Goldsmith's verse. Note, too, Goldsmith's frequent use of symmetrical patterns of syntax. Wordsworth is much more self-effacing and unassertive: the general effect of his blank verse and run-on lines is to help present Michael's story as something which is personal and individual, not as something to be pronounced upon in terms of some logical and systematic way of looking at life in general. Comparatively speaking, Goldsmith's verse is formal, and Wordsworth's colloquial or conversational.

These are, of course, extreme examples. But they help us to see, for example, that by skilfully mixing end-stopped and run-on lines in a rhyming poem, a superb craftsman like Yeats can achieve a fine balance between the presentation of himself as a professional poet, *and* as a human being passionately arguing with himself in the medium of everyday speech. This balance between end-stopped and run-on lines, between the formal and the colloquial, is apparent in the lines from 'Leda and the Swan' which were quoted in Chapter 1 ('Diction') and in such poems as 'No Second Troy', which begins thus:

> Why should I blame her that she filled my days
> With misery, or that she would of late
> Have taught to ignorant men most violent ways,
> Or hurled the little streets upon the great,
> Had they but courage equal to desire?

(iii) Foregrounded Style

The term 'foregrounded style' is extremely useful in discussing the degree of patterning in a piece of literature. A 'foregrounded' style, or manner of writing (the term is borrowed from Linguistics) is one which thrusts itself upon the reader's attention, like a prominent object in the foreground. In other words, it draws attention to itself *as* a style, and therefore to the author's work as a piece of literary craftsmanship created by a literary craftsman. A highly formal style such as Dr. Johnson's can be described as 'foregrounded', because its symmetrical patterns of syntax thrust themselves upon our attention. Not all foregrounded styles are 'formal' in this sense of the word, however, as we may see from the opening lines of Gerard Manley Hopkins' poem 'That Nature is a Heraclitean Fire ...':

> Cloud-puffball, torn tufts, tossed pillows flaunt forth, then chevy on an air-
> Built thoroughfare: heaven-roysterers, in gay-gangs they throng; they glitter
>   in marches.
> Down roughcast, down dazzling whitewash, wherever an elm arches,
> Shivelights and shadowtackle in long lashes lace, lance, and pair.

Hopkins' poetic style is heavily foregrounded, and its highly-wrought patterns distance his most personal statements. Lawrence's prose style, in the following example of narrated interior monologue from *The Rainbow*, is as colloquial and unassertive as Wordsworth's poetic style in 'Michael', and with similar effects:

> For Anna the moment was critical. She kept herself aloof, and watched him. He talked to her, but with a little indifference, since he was scarcely aware of her. So, then she did not affect him. Here was a new turn of affairs! He was better attractive, nevertheless. She liked him better than the ordinary mute, half-effaced, half-subdued man she usually knew him to be. So, he was blossoming out into his real self! It piqued her. Very good, let him blossom! She liked a new turn of affairs. He was a strange man come home to her.

A highly important traditional kind of foregrounded style is that used in epic poems to 'elevate' the subject-matter. As M. H. Abrams says in his *A Glossary of Literary Terms*:

> An epic poem is a ceremonial performance, and is narrated in a ceremonial style which is deliberately distanced from ordinary speech and proportioned to the grandeur and formality of the heroic subject matter and epic architecture. Hence Milton's 'grand style'—his Latinate diction and stylized syntax, his sonorous lists of names and wide-ranging allusions, and his imitation of Homer's epic similes and epithets.

Epic elevation is discussed in the chapter which follows, as an introduction to the highly important and often-used literary techniques of mock-heroic deflation, and 'bathos'.

Exercise 1

[Christian Example]

SHYLOCK: ... He hath disgraced me, and hindered me half a million; laughed at my losses, mocked at my gains, scorned my nation, thwarted my bargains, cooled my friends, heated mine enemies; and what's his reason? I am a Jew. Hath not a Jew eyes? Hath not a Jew hands, organs, dimensions, senses, affections, passions? Fed with the same food, hurt with the same weapons, subject to the same diseases, healed by the same means, warmed and cooled by the same winter and summer, as a Christian is? If you prick us, do we not bleed? If you tickle us, do we not laugh? If you poison us, do we not die? And if you wrong us, shall we not revenge? If we are like you in the rest, we will resemble you in that. If a Jew wrong a Christian, what is his humility? Revenge. If a Christian wrong a Jew, what should his sufferance be by Christian example? Why, revenge. The villainy you teach me, I will execute, and it shall go hard but I will better the instruction.

> William Shakespeare: from *The Merchant of Venice.*

'What is his humility?': 'what is the Christian's "humility"?'; 'what should his sufferance be?': 'what allowance should the Jew make?'; 'but I will': 'if I do not'.

The patterns of syntax employed by Shakespeare in his plays and poems show that he received an extremely thorough grounding in traditional rhetoric, like any other Elizabethan grammar-school boy. Shylock's famous speech is a striking example of Shakespeare's use of patterns of this kind.

What are Shylock's arguments? What do the patterns of syntax contribute to the force of these arguments?

As an aid to answering these questions, the reader is recommended to write down the speech in the tabular form used earlier to clarify the patterning in Dickens's description of the Chuzzlewits (p. 85). What kinds of pattern then emerge?

Exercise 2

[Don Juan vs. the Devil]

THE DEVIL: ... I could give you a thousand instances; but they all come to the same thing: the power that governs the earth is not the power of Life but of Death; and the inner need that has served Life to the effort of organizing itself into the human being is not the need for higher life but for a more efficient engine of destruction. The plague, the famine, the earthquake, the tempest were too spasmodic in their action; the tiger and crocodile were too easily satiated and not cruel enough: something more constantly, more ruthlessly, more ingeniously destructive was needed; and that something was Man, the inventor of the rack, the stake, the gallows, the electric chair; of sword and gun and poison gas: above all, of justice, duty, patriotism, and all the other isms by which even those who are clever enough to be humanely disposed are persuaded to become the most destructive of all the destroyers.

DON JUAN: Pshaw! all this is old. Your weak side, my diabolic friend, is that you have always been a gull: you take Man at his own valuation. Nothing would flatter him more than your opinion of him. He loves to think of himself as bold and bad. He is neither one nor the other: he is only a coward. Call him tyrant, murderer, pirate, bully; and he will adore you, and swagger about with the consciousness of having the blood of the old sea kings in his veins. Call him liar and thief; and he will only take an action against you for libel. But call him coward; and he will go mad with rage: he will face death to outface that stinging truth. Man gives every reason for his conduct save one, every excuse for his crimes save one, every plea for his safety save one: and that one is his cowardice. Yet all his civilization is founded on his cowardice, on his abject tameness, which he calls his respectability. There are limits to what a mule or an ass will stand; but Man will suffer himself to be degraded until his vileness becomes so loathsome to his oppressors that they themselves are forced to reform it.

THE DEVIL: Precisely. And these are the creatures in whom you discover what you call a Life Force!

DON JUAN: Yes; for now comes the most surprising part of the whole business.

THE STATUE: What's that?

DON JUAN: Why, that you can make any of these cowards brave by simply putting an idea into his head.

George Bernard Shaw: from *Man & Superman*

Describe the part played by patterns of syntax in the development of each character's argument. Do you detect any flaws in the logic of either speaker?

Exercise 3

The world of Emily Brontë's *Wuthering Heights* is a world of violently opposed extremes in the character-types depicted and the settings in which they move. This basic dualism is strongly reinforced from time to time by the figurative language and the symmetrical patterns of syntax which the characters are made to employ when speaking.

In the first extract given below from *Wuthering Heights*, Catherine Earnshaw describes her love for Heathcliff; in the second, her daughter Catherine compares her idea of heaven with that of Heathcliff's son. Both of these speeches, like Shylock's in the previous exercise, are found particularly memorable by most readers of literature. This is probably because they too make full use of the formal rhetorical devices of parallel and antithesis.

Clarify the syntactical patterning in these two speeches by writing them down in tabular form, then describe in detail what contributions both patterning and figurative language make to the total effect of each passage.

(Trying to re-write a passage in a *less* patterned way by altering the sequence of particular groups of words can help us to see what effects the original patterns have, without in any way changing the original words and their connotations.)

(i) '... It would degrade me to marry Heathcliff now; so he shall never know how I love him; and that, not because he's handsome, Nelly, but because he's more myself than I am. Whatever our souls are made of, his and mine are the same, and Linton's is as different as a moonbeam from lightning, or frost from fire.

*   *   *

I cannot express it; but surely you and everybody have a notion that there is, or should be, an existence of yours beyond you. What were the use of my creation if I were entirely constrained here? My great miseries in this world have been Heathcliff's miseries, and I watched and felt each from the beginning; my great thought in living is himself. If all else perished, and *he* remained, I should still continue to be; and, if all else remained, and he were annihilated, the Universe would turn to a mighty stranger. I should not seem a part of it. My love for Linton is like the foliage in the woods. Time will change it, I'm well aware, as winter changes the trees. My love for Heathcliff resembles the eternal rocks beneath— a source of little visible delight, but necessary. Nelly, I *am* Heathcliff—he's always, always in my mind—not as a pleasure, any more than I am always a pleasure to myself—but as my own being—so, don't talk of our separation again—it is impracticable; and—'
  She paused, and hid her face in the folds of my gown...

(ii) 'One time, however, we were near quarrelling. He said the pleasantest manner of spending a hot July day was lying from morning till evening on a bank of heath in the middle of the moors, with the bees humming dreamily about among the bloom, and the larks singing high up over head, and the blue sky and bright sun shining steadily and cloudlessly. That was his most perfect idea of heaven's happiness. Mine was rocking in a rustling green tree, with a west wind blowing, and bright, white clouds flitting rapidly above; and not only larks, but throstles, and blackbirds, and linnets, and cuckoos pouring out music on every side, and the moors seen at a distance, broken into cool dusky dells; but close by, great swells of long grass undulating in waves to the breeze; and woods and sounding water, and the whole world awake and wild with joy. He wanted all to lie in an ecstacy of peace; I wanted all to sparkle, and dance in a glorious jubilee.
  'I said his heaven would be only half alive, and he said mine would be drunk; I said I should fall asleep in his, and he said he could not breathe in mine, and began to grow very snappish. At last, we agreed to try both as soon as the right weather came; and then we kissed each other and were friends.'

Exercise 4

[The High Court of Chancery]

  The raw afternoon is rawest, and the dense fog is densest, and the muddy streets are muddiest, near that leaden-headed old obstruction, appropriate ornament for the threshold of a leaden-headed old corporation: Temple Bar. And hard by

Temple Bar, in Lincoln's Inn Hall, at the very heart of the fog, sits the Lord High Chancellor in his High Court of Chancery.

Never can there come fog too thick, never can there come mud and mire too deep, to assort with the groping and floundering condition which this High Court of Chancery, most pestilent of hoary sinners, holds, this day, in the sight of heaven and earth.

On such an afternoon, if ever, the Lord High Chancellor ought to be sitting here—as here he is—with a foggy glory round his head, softly fenced in with crimson cloth and curtains, addressed by a large advocate with great whiskers, a little voice, and an interminable brief, and outwardly directing his contemplation to the lantern in the roof, where he can see nothing but fog. On such an afternoon, some score of members of the High Court of Chancery bar ought to be—as here they are—mistily engaged in one of the ten thousand stages of an endless cause, tripping one another up on slippery precedents, groping knee-deep in technicalities, running their goat-hair and horse-hair warded heads against walls of words, and making a pretence of equity with serious faces, as players might. On such an afternoon, the various solicitors in the cause, some two or three of whom have inherited it from their fathers, who made a fortune by it, ought to be—as are they not?—ranged in a line, in a long matted well (but you might look in vain for Truth at the bottom of it), between the registrar's red table and the silk gowns, with bills, cross-bills, answers, rejoinders, injunctions, affidavits, issues, references to masters, masters' reports, mountains of costly nonsense, piled before them. Well may the court be dim, with wasting candles here and there; well may the fog hang heavy in it, as if it would never get out; well may the stained glass windows lose their colour, and admit no light of day into the place; well may the uninitiated from the streets, who peep in through the glass panes in the door, be deterred from entrance by its owlish aspect, and by the drawl languidly echoing to the roof from the padded dais where the Lord High Chancellor looks into the lantern that has no light in it, and where the attendant wigs are all stuck in a fog-bank! This is the Court of Chancery; which has its decaying houses and its blighted lands in every shire; which has its worn-out lunatic in every madhouse, and its dead in every churchyard; which has its ruined suitor, with his slipshod heels and threadbare dress, borrowing and begging through the round of every man's acquaintance; which gives to moneyed might, the means abundantly of wearying out the right; which so exhausts finances, patience, courage, hope; so overthrows the brain and breaks the heart; that there is not an honourable man among its practitioners who would not give—who does not often give—the warning, 'Suffer any wrong that can be done you, rather than come here!'

Charles Dickens: from *Bleak House*

'High Court of Chancery': this Court dealt with matters of 'equity' such as disputed wills. Its proceedings were notoriously long drawn out and costly.

'The cause': 'the case'; 'lantern': 'a recessed skylight'; 'suitor': 'plaintiff'.

Dickens puts his London fog to highly complex uses. Just as London symbolizes (i.e. represents) England, so its fog symbolizes the physical confusion, dirt and misery of the life of the whole nation. By placing the Court of Chancery at the heart of this actual and symbolic fog, Dickens suggests that the metaphorical 'fog' of legal arguments is not only akin to it, but in fact gives rise to it and what it represents.

Write detailed comments on this and other effects achieved by Dickens's patterns of syntax in the extract.

Exercise 5

The Hourglass

Do but consider this small dust,
Here running in the glass,
   By atoms moved;
Could you believe that this
The body was
   Of one that loved?
And in his Mistress' flame, playing like a fly,
   Turned to cinders by her eye?
      Yes; and in death, as life, unblest,
        To have't expressed,
Even ashes of lovers find no rest.
Ben Jonson

The last three lines of Jonson's poem might be paraphrased as follows: 'Yes; and he was given no blessing when he died, just as he had received none when he was alive, in order to illustrate the fact that rejected lovers go on suffering even after death.'

By playing on the words 'unblest' and 'rest', Jonson ingeniously fuses two commonplaces: a lover is distracted and cannot sleep if his mistress refuses to bless him with her favours; a dead person cannot rest in peace if he is buried without a proper religious blessing. A third commonplace is present by implication: a lover will die if spurned by his mistress.

'Ashes' signifies both the 'small dust' to which this particular unfortunate lover has allegedly been reduced, and the mortal remains ('dust and ashes') of rejected lovers generally. The word 'ashes' should receive the main spoken emphasis in the last line of Jonson's poem and in that of Coleridge's version which follows:

The Hour-Glass

O think, fair maid! these sands that pass
In slender threads adown this glass,
Were once the body of some swain,

> Who lov'd too well and lov'd in vain,
> And let one soft sigh heave thy breast,
> That not in life alone unblest
> E'en lovers' ashes find no rest.
>   Samuel Taylor Coleridge

What has Coleridge left out? What has he added? What changes in diction and patterning has he introduced? What are the differences in overall meaning between his poem and Jonson's original?

Compare and contrast the two poems, drawing particular attention to the changes in tone brought about by Coleridge's alterations to Jonson's verse-patterning.

7
Epic Elevation, Mock-Heroic Deflation, and Bathos

Although elevated language may be used to invite respect and admiration, it is equally often used to invite the complete opposite: disrespect and even contempt. This exactly contrary purpose is clearly one which it is highly important for us to be able to recognize, for we may otherwise completely misinterpret an author's intended meaning.

The use of elevated diction by authors who wish to invite disrespect and ridicule is at its most obvious in what is called 'mock-heroic' or 'mock-epic' writing. 'Bathos', which is one of the most distinctive features of this kind of writing, is also commonly used by many novelists and poets who wish to achieve similar effects to theirs, as we shall see. But before these topics can be discussed, something needs to be said about genuine epic poetry.

Epic poems are today as obsolete as formal odes, though epic tales themselves live on vigorously in the form of countless 'Wild West' films (where the appropriate elevation is provided by the musical accompaniment), just as the tradition of the late-eighteenth-century 'Gothic novel' lives on in the guise of countless 'horror' movies.

An epic poem is a long narrative poem which describes the adventures of a *hero*, a figure of great historical and mythical importance to his tribe or race. The most famous Western European epics are the *Iliad* and the *Odyssey* of Homer, and the *Aeneid* of Virgil. The epic poet uses elevated diction in order to dignify and ennoble the central characters and to render supremely important the events in which they are involved. Here, for example, is a description of Hector, the mightiest of the Trojan warriors, taken from Pope's translation of the *Iliad*:

> Now rushing in the furious Chief appears,
> Gloomy as Night! and shakes two shining Spears:
> A dreadful Gleam from his bright Armour came,
> And from his Eye-balls flash'd the living Flame;
> He moves a God, resistless in his Course,
> And seems a Match for more than mortal Force.

The last two lines make plain what is implied in the previous four. Hector 'moves (like) a God'. Like epic heroes generally, he is being presented as an awesomely superhuman figure, a superman.

A mock-epic or mock-heroic poem imitates the elevated style of the proper epic, but applies it to commonplace contemporary characters and actions. Its author's purpose is usually to ridicule these characters and actions, for the effect of describing trivial things in elevated diction is to make them appear more trivial still. Contemporary life and manners are made to appear petty and 'degenerate' by being unfavourably contrasted with the heroic life of antiquity. In 'The Rape of the Lock', which is one of the most famous of English mock-heroic poems, Pope writes about an actual incident which caused a scandal in polite society, the cutting off of a young lady's lock of hair by one of her admirers. By using the highly elevated diction appropriate to an epic, Pope ridicules the exaggerated importance which the young lady's family and friends attached to the incident, and at the same time satirizes the foibles of fashionable society generally.

One of the poem's most famous episodes is an imaginary battle between the young fops and young beauties of the day, who are satirized by being likened to superhuman heroic warriors like Hector. In the following short extract from this scene, Thalestris, the leader of the women, is initially presented in the elevated diction appropriate to a mighty warrior. She is quickly made to appear absurd, however, when Pope describes the genteel weapons and armour of her 'army': fans, silk gowns, and whalebone corsets:

> To Arms, to Arms! the bold Thalestris cries,
> And swift as Lightning to the Combate flies.
> All side in Parties, and begin th'Attack;
> Fans clap, Silks russle, and tough Whalebones crack . . .

The comparison of undistinguished persons to the mighty heroes of the past makes them appear both pretentious and absurd: it 'deflates' them. The central device used in this mock-heroic process of 'deflation' is that of deliberate *bathos* or anticlimax, a noticeable drop from elevated diction to commonplace or even vulgar diction, as in the drop from words like 'arms', 'bold', 'lightning' and 'combat', with all their connotations of heroic hardiness, to words like 'fans', 'silks', 'russle' and 'whalebones', with all their connotations of trivial feminine fashions and foibles. Pope's other famous mock-heroic poem *The Dunciad*, which satirizes the literary hacks of the day, provides a still more condensed example of the deflationary use of bathos in two lines describing the startling re-appearance of Smedley, who has been stuck in the mud at the bottom of the River Thames and given up for lost:

> Sudden, a burst of thunder shook the flood.
> Lo! Smedley rose, in majesty of mud!

The elevated epic diction of the first line is deflated by the last word of the second, and the unfortunate Smedley with it. The phrase 'majesty of mud' itself is worth our remembering as a pithy example of the mock-heroic use of bathos: the elevated word 'majesty', with all its connotations of power and grandeur, is immediately deflated by the commonplace word 'mud', with all its connotations of dirt and indignity.

A similarly condensed example of mock-heroic bathos is worth remembering from Dryden's 'Macflecknoe', which was the model for Pope's *Dunciad*. In one line of Dryden's poem, unsuccessful authors and their works are described as:

> Martyrs of pies, and relics of the bum.

Their unsold works, in other words, have been torn up and used for covering pies, and as lavatory-paper. These neglected authors are elevated by being referred to as 'martyrs', who are religious *heroes*, and their unsold pages are elevated by being referred to as 'relics': the personal items which originally belonged to these heroic, saintly and legendary figures, and which are therefore now regarded with the greatest reverence. These elevated words, together with all their noble connotations, are quickly deflated by the vulgar words 'pies' and 'bum'.

Although authors usually use the mock-heroic technique of deliberate bathos in order to deflate the pretensions of their real or imaginary characters, they sometimes use it to deflate what they regard as the pretentiousness of elevated language itself. Here are two examples of bathos used for this purpose, which suggest that the technique is one which changes little over the years:

> Now the rake Hesperus had called for his breeches, and having well rubbed his drowsy eyes, prepared to dress himself for night; by whose example his brother rakes on earth likewise leave those beds in which they had slept away the day. Now Thetis the good housewife, began to put on the pot, in order to regale the good man Phoebus after his daily labours were over. In vulgar language, it was in the evening when Joseph attended his lady's orders.
>
> Henry Fielding: *Joseph Andrews*, 1742.

Writers usually introduce the classical gods such as Hesperus (the evening-star, hence the goddess Venus), Thetis (the sea-god's daughter) and Phoebus (the sun-god Apollo) in order to elevate and dignify their descriptions of dawns and sunsets. Here, instead, Fielding first devalues these supernatural figures by reducing them to the level of rakes and rustics, and then dismisses them altogether, preferring 'vulgar language' to such misplaced elevation.

Bathos is used for exactly the same purpose in a description of evening by Spike Milligan in *A Dustbin of Milligan* (1961). Just as Fielding introduces Hesperus, Thetis and Phoebus, so Milligan introduces the figures of Castor, Pollux and Andromeda. Castor and Pollux, who in classical mythology were the twin sons of Zeus and Leda, have given their names to the two brightest stars in the constellation of Gemini. Andromeda, descended from Zeus and Danaë, has also given her name to a constellation. Spike Milligan first elevates his description of evening and the coming of night by using traditional heroic references to 'the shields of a victorious army' and to the illustrious descendants of almighty Zeus, and then introduces a crashing bathos in the last six words:

> The clouds look like the shields of a victorious army, then suddenly the sun is gone and lo! the curtain of night is down The master tailor sews his bejewelled charges to the black canopy of the heavens. On high they cluster—the pendants of the constellation Castor, Pollux, Andromeda all glitter in the velvet darkness, like oily chips on boiled haddock.

Bathos may of course be quite unintentional, as in the famous couplet on the death of Queen Victoria:

> Dust to dust, and ashes to ashes,
> Into the tomb the Great Queen dashes.

Here, the awesome words of the Anglican service for The Burial of the Dead ('earth to earth, ashes to ashes, dust to dust'), together with the solemn connotations of the words 'tomb', 'great' and 'queen' are rendered absurd by the introduction of the word 'dashes'. In context, this suggests an extremely undignified and unqueenly haste on Queen Victoria's part to take her rightful place in Heaven.

Again, bathos may be accidental. I remember being amused, as a schoolboy, and long before I had heard of such things as 'bathos' and 'mock-heroic techniques', to discover on a library shelf three imposing volumes in identical binding in the following order: *The Glory That Was Greece*; *The Grandeur That Was Rome*; *The Story Of The Co-Operative Wholesale Society*.

Although epic poems are no longer written, and although the great age of the English mock-epic poem was the age of Dryden and Pope, mock-heroic techniques have been employed by such important twentieth-century authors as T. S. Eliot and James Joyce, and an awareness of these techniques is essential to an understanding of some of their major works.

In 'The Waste Land', for example, T. S. Eliot continually invokes

the departed grandeur of Elizabethan England in order to emphasize
the triviality and sordidness of twentieth-century life in London. One
of the ways in which he does this is by quoting from Elizabethan
poetry. Just as Pope and Dryden in their mock-epic poems used direct
quotations from the *Aeneid*, the *Iliad* and the *Odyssey* in order first
to elevate their contemporary subject-matter and then to deflate it, so
Eliot uses quotations from Shakespeare, Spenser, Milton and Marvell.
Here are two examples, both taken from the section of Eliot's poem
entitled 'The Fire Sermon':

> Sweet Thames, run softly, till I end my song.
> The river bears no empty bottles, sandwich papers ...
>
> But at my back from time to time I hear
> The sound of horns and motors ...

The first line in the first quotation is taken directly from Edmund
Spenser's famous 'Prothalamion', written in 1596 to celebrate a great
aristocratic marriage; the first line in the second quotation is adapted
from Andrew Marvell's famous poem 'To His Coy Mistress'. In each
example, Eliot employs bathos. The quotations, though n)t in elevated
diction themselves, serve to remind us of the grandeur that was Elizabethan England and the glory that was Elizabethan poetry. The commonplace diction of the second lines ('empty bottles, sandwich
papers'; 'horns and motors') works in exactly the same way as Pope's
'mud' and Dryden's 'pies' and 'bum'. Contemporary trivialities are
made to appear still more trivial by being compared with the achievements of the heroic past. Interestingly enough, the early drafts of 'The
Waste Land' contained a long section modelled on Pope's 'The Rape
of the Lock' which was deleted from the published version, and which
shows that Eliot was a keen student of Pope's mock-heroic techniques. Eliot also uses quotations from other writers such as Dante
and Virgil to achieve similar effects in 'The Waste Land', and towards
the end of the section of his poem which is entitled 'The Fire Sermon'
the heroic world of Wagner's *The Twilight of the Gods* is alluded to
in order to emphasize the pitifully sordid circumstances in which three
girls from modern London lost their virginity.

James Joyce's novel *Ulysses*, although it describes the lives of three
main characters in Dublin on a single day in 1904, is modelled on
Homer's *Odyssey*, as the title deliberately points out. Although Joyce
often uses mock-heroic techniques in this novel, their intention is too
complicated to be commented on without distortion here. Instead, I
shall complete this chapter by quoting two passages from Joyce's

earlier novel *A Portrait of the Artist as a Young Man*, in which something very like the mock-heroic technique is continually used to deflate the delusions of grandeur of the central character, the would-be artist Stephen Dedalus.

Throughout the novel, Stephen's elevated and self-indulgent fantasies are derived from his avid reading of literature, rather than any experience of real life. Joyce continually draws attention to this by following a passage of Stephen's narrated interior monologue, written in a self-consciously 'literary' style, with a deflating passage of authorial narration written in a much more prosaic style. In the following extract the schoolboy Stephen is lying in bed in the school hospital, suffering from a slight fever, and contemplating his own death and funeral with a good deal of self-pitying enjoyment:

> He wanted to cry quietly but not for himself: for the words, so beautiful and sad, like music. The bell! The bell! Farewell! O farewell!
> The cold sunlight was weaker and Brother Michael was standing at his bedside with a bowl of beef-tea.

The 'words, so beautiful and sad' which Stephen quotes come from a sentimental ballad in which the dying narrator asks to be buried 'in the old churchyard'. Joyce quietly deflates this high-flown day-dream by introducing the commonplace 'bowl of beef-tea', which is a prosaic reminder that an ounce of Brother Michael's practical Christianity is worth a ton of such literary fantasies. This small incident provides the key to a number of others which later deflate the adolescent Stephen's conception of himself as an artistic 'priest of the eternal imagination' by drawing attention to its complete lack of charitable concern for others. 'Not for himself' is of course ironical.

Our next quotation contains the last paragraph of the fourth section of *A Portrait of the Artist as a Young Man,* and the first paragraph of the section which immediately follows it. As will be seen, Joyce employs a sharply contrasted diction in each paragraph:

> He climbed to the crest of the sandhill and gazed about him. Evening had fallen. A rim of the young moon cleft the pale waste of skyline, the rim of a silver hoop embedded in grey sand; and the tide was flowing in fast to the land with a low whisper of her waves, islanding a few last figures in distant pools.

> He drained his third cup of watery tea to the dregs and set to chewing the crusts of fried bread that were scattered near him, staring into the dark pool of the jar. The yellow dripping had been scooped out like a boghole and the pool under it brought back to his memory the dark turf-coloured water of the bath in Clongowes.

The first paragraph describes the evening scene as it presents itself to Stephen's imagination. The diction is distinctly literary, even 'poetical'. The evening is a hackneyed subject for poetical musings, as we are reminded by the cliché 'Evening had fallen'. Both the moon ('the *young* moon') and the tide ('the *whisper* of *her* waves') are personified, and the rim of the moon is metaphorically likened, in another poetical cliché, to the rim of a silver hoop. The adjectives 'pale', 'silver' and 'grey' are also clichés of picturesque writing in the nineteenth-century Romantic tradition, especially of the late-nineteenth-century Irish 'Celtic Twilight' variety.

The second paragraph describes the following morning as it presents itself to the detached narrator. Here the sordid realities of breakfast in the Dedalus household are used to deflate Stephen's poetical imaginings. Stephen 'drains' his third cup of tea and 'chews the crusts' of fried bread in a most unpoetical manner. The crusts of fried bread are 'scattered' about the table in a slovenly fashion, and the jar of dripping has been brutally 'scooped out'. The use of words with unpleasant connotations, such as 'dregs', 'crusts', 'yellow dripping' and 'boghole' is (once again) remarkably similar to Pope's use of 'mud' and Dryden's use of 'pies' and 'bum'. The 'dark pool' in the jar of dripping and the memory of the unpleasantly dark bath-water at Clongowes School take up the reference to 'distant pools' in the first paragraph and deflate its literary pretensions. The main effect here is to show that Stephen is using literature as a means of escape from a reality which he is not prepared to try to change.

It is worth noting here as a last example of bathos that Evelyn Waugh, in his travel-book *Labels*, uses it to deflate much the same kind of hackneyed 'picturesque' writing as Joyce alludes to in the first of the two paragraphs just discussed:

> I do not think I shall ever forget the sight of Etna at sunset; the mountain almost invisible in a blur of pastel grey, glowing on the top and then repeating its shape, as though reflected, in a wisp of grey smoke, with the whole horizon behind radiant with pink light, fading gently into a grey pastel sky. Nothing I have ever seen in Art or Nature was quite so revolting.

What, finally, can be said about the general effects of using elevated diction ironically, in conjunction with mock-heroic deflation and bathos? It should be clear that these techniques, however comical, are used by authors in order to make moral evaluations and moral distinctions. Their purpose is didactic. Elevated diction, used sincerely, invites us to value highly what the author himself values highly. Ironic

elevation, mock-heroic deflation and bathos serve the opposite purpose. They invite us to see that what may appear to be highly valuable
is 'in fact' (in the author's opinion, that is) both worthless and trivial.

Exercise 1

The following extract is from John Gay's *Trivia; Or the Art of Walking the Streets of London* (1716). It appears towards the end of Book III
of Gay's poem, which is entitled 'Of Walking the Streets by Night'.
In this book Gay describes the nocturnal hazards of contemporary
London life: quarrelling drivers, pickpockets, jostling crowds, prosti-
tutes, gangs of delinquents, and so on (not much has changed). The
passage below describes a fire and the way in which neighbouring
houses were blown up with gunpowder ('barrelled grain') to prevent
it spreading.

The 'Dardan hero' is Aeneas. What episode from Book II of *The
Aeneid* is alluded to in this line? What other allusions of this kind occur
in the extract?

Comment on the various mock-heroic techniques employed in the
extract and describe the effects which Gay achieves by their use.

How would you describe Gay's satirical tone here?

> But hark! distress with screaming voice draws nigher,
> And wakes the slumbering street with cries of fire.
> At first a glowing red enwraps the skies,
> And borne by winds the scattering sparks arise;
> From beam to beam the fierce contagion spreads;
> The spiry flames now lift aloft their heads,
> Through the burst sash a blazing deluge pours,
> And splitting tiles descend in rattling showers.
> Now with thick crowds th' enlightened pavement swarms,
> The fireman sweats beneath his crooked arms,
> A leathern casque his venturous head defends,
> Boldly he climbs where thickest smoke ascends;
> Moved by the mother's streaming eyes and prayers,
> The helpless infant through the flame he bears,
> With no less virtue, than through hostile fire
> The Dardan hero bore his aged sire.
> See forceful engines spout their levelled streams,
> To quench the blaze that runs along the beams;
> The grappling hook plucks rafters from the walls,
> And heaps on heaps the smoky ruin falls.
> Blown by strong winds the fiery tempest roars,
> Bears down new walls and pours along the floors;
> The heavens are all ablaze, the face of night
> Is covered with a sanguine dreadful light:

'Twas such a light involved thy towers, O Rome,
The dire presage of mighty Caesar's doom,
When the sun veiled in rust his mourning head,
And frightful prodigies the skies o'erspread.
Hark! the drum thunders! far, ye crowds, retire:
Behold! the ready match is tipped with fire,
The nitrous store is laid, the smutty train
With running blaze awakes the barreled grain;
Flames sudden wrap the walls; with sullen sound
The shattered pile sinks on the smoky ground.
So when the years shall have revolved the date,
Th' inevitable hour of Naples' fate,
Her sapped foundations shall with thunders shake,
And heave and toss upon the sulfurous lake;
Earth's womb at once the fiery flood shall rend,
And in th'abyss her plunging towers descend.
   Consider, reader, what fatigues I've known,
The toils, the perils of the wintry town;
What riots seen, what bustling crowds I bored,
How oft I crossed where carts and coaches roared;
Yet shall I bless my labors, if mankind
Their future safety from my dangers find.
Thus the bold traveler (inured to toil,
Whose steps have printed Asia's desert soil,
The barbarous Arabs' haunt; or shivering crossed
Dark Greenland's mountains of eternal frost;
Whom providence in length of years restores
To the wished harbor of his native shores)
Sets forth his journals to the public view,
To caution, by his woes, the wandering crew.
                              John Gay: from *Trivia*

Exercise 2

Ode on the Death of a Favorite Cat

'Twas on a lofty vase's side,
Where China's gayest art had dyed
   The azure flowers that blow,
Demurest of the tabby kind,
The pensive Selima reclined,
   Gazed on the lake below.

Her conscious tail her joy declared;
The fair round face, the snowy beard,
   The velvet of her paws,
Her coat, that with the tortoise vies,
Her ears of jet, and emerald eyes,
   She saw; and purred applause.

Still had she gazed; but 'midst the tide
Two angel forms were seen to glide,
    The Genii of the stream:
Their scaly armour's Tyrian hue
Through richest purple to the view
    Betrayed a golden gleam.

The hapless nymph with wonder saw:
A whisker first and then a claw,
    With many an ardent wish,
She stretched in vain to reach the prize.
What female heart can gold despise?
    What cat's averse to fish?

Presumptuous maid! with looks intent
Again she stretched, again she bent,
    Nor knew the gulf between.
(Malignant Fate sat by, and smiled)
The slippery verge her feet beguiled,
    She tumbled headlong in.

Eight times emerging from the flood
She mewed to every wat'ry god,
    Some speedy aid to send.
No dolphin came, no nereid stirred;
Nor cruel Tom nor Susan heard.
    A favourite has no friend!

From hence, ye beauties, undeceived,
Know, one false step is ne'er retrieved,
    And be with caution bold.
Not all that tempts your wandering eyes
And heedless hearts is lawful prize.
    Nor all that glisters, gold.

                                   Thomas Gray

'Tom ... Susan': names of servants.

Describe the various means by which Gray elevates the incident, and comment on his use of bathos.

Does Gray use these standard mock-heroic techniques in order to invite ridicule of the cat? How serious is the poem as a whole? Is it any more than an elegant performance? Taking into account every aspect of the poem, including its degree of patterning, how would you describe its tone?

Exercise 3

[A Gruesome Spectacle]

The last farewell was affecting in the extreme. From the belfries far and near the funereal deathbell tolled unceasingly while all around the gloomy precincts rolled the ominous warning of a hundred muffled drums punctuated by the hollow booming of pieces of ordnance. The deafening claps of thunder and the dazzling flashes of lightning which lit up the ghastly scene testified that the artillery of heaven had lent its supernatural pomp to the already gruesome spectacle.

*   *   *

Quite an excellent repast consisting of rashers and eggs, fried steak and onions, done to a nicety, delicious hot breakfast rolls and invigorating tea had been considerately provided by the authorities for the consumption of the central figure of the tragedy who was in capital spirits when prepared for death and evinced the keenest interest in the proceedings from beginning to end but he, with an abnegation rare in these our times, rose nobly to the occasion and expressed the dying wish (immediately acceded to) that the meal should be divided in aliquot parts among the members of the sick and indigent roomkeepers' association as a token of his regard and esteem. The *nec* and *non plus ultra* of emotion were reached when the blushing bride elect burst her way through the serried ranks of the bystanders and flung herself upon the muscular bosom of him who was about to be launched into eternity for her sake. The hero folded her willowy form in a loving embrace murmuring fondly *Sheila, my own.* Encouraged by this use of her christian name she kissed passionately all the various suitable areas of his person which the decencies of prison garb permitted her ardour to reach. She swore to him as they mingled the salt streams of their tears that she would cherish his memory, that she would never forget her hero boy who went to his death with a song on his lips as if he were but going to a hurling match in Clonturk park.

*   *   *

A most romantic incident occurred when a handsome young Oxford graduate, noted for his chivalry towards the fair sex, stepped forward and, presenting his visiting card, bankbook and genealogical tree solicited the hand of the hapless young lady, requesting her to name the day, and was accepted on the spot. Every lady in the audience was presented with a tasteful souvenir of the occasion in the shape of a skull and crossbones brooch, a timely and generous act which evoked a fresh outburst of emotion: and when the gallant young Oxonian (the bearer, by the way, of one of the most timehonoured names in Albion's history) placed on the finger of his blushing *fiancée* an expensive engagement ring with emeralds set in the form of a four-leaved shamrock excitement knew no bounds. Nay, even the stern provostmarshal, lieutenantcolonel Tomkin–Maxwell ffrenchmullan Tomlinson, who presided on the sad occasion, he who had blown a considerable number of sepoys from the cannonmouth without flinching, could not now restrain his natural emotion. With his mailed gauntlet he brushed away a furtive tear and was overheard by those privileged burghers who happened to be in his immediate *entourage* to murmur to himself in a faltering undertone:

—God blimey if she aint a clinker, that there bleeding tart. Blimey it makes me kind of bleeding cry, straight, it does, when I sees her cause I thinks of my old mashtub what's waiting for me down Limehouse way.

James Joyce: from *Ulysses*

The passage above is a considerably abridged extract from the 'Cyclops' episode of *Ulysses*, in which Joyce employs on an extended scale the standard mock-heroic technique of alternating elevation and deflation: vulgar gossip in a Dublin bar is interwoven with commentaries on the topics discussed, each commentary parodying a different kind of elevated style.

Conversation having turned to a regular topic, the execution of Irish political heroes and martyrs, Joyce inserts the description of one such execution during the period of British rule, written in a fantastically inflated and cliché-ridden style.

What are the objects of Joyce's satire here? How would you describe his tone?

Exercise 4

Heaven

Fish (fly-replete, in depth of June,
Dawdling away their wat'ry noon)
Ponder deep wisdom, dark or clear,
Each secret fishy hope or fear.
Fish say, they have their Stream and Pond;
But is there anything Beyond?
This life cannot be All, they swear,
For how unpleasant, if it were!
One may not doubt that, somehow, Good
Shall come of Water and of Mud;
And, sure, the reverent eye must see
A Purpose in Liquidity.
We darkly know, by Faith we cry,
The future is not Wholly Dry.
Mud unto mud!—Death eddies near—
Not here the appointed End, not here!
But somewhere, beyond Space and Time,
Is wetter water, slimier slime!
And there (they trust) there swimmeth One
Who swam ere rivers were begun,
Immense, of fishy form and mind,
Squamous, omnipotent, and kind;
And under that Almighty Fin,
The littlest fish may enter in.
Oh! never fly conceals a hook,
Fish say, in the Eternal Brook,
But more than mundane weeds are there,
And mud, celestially fair;
Fat caterpillars drift around,
And Paradisal grubs are found;
Unfading moths, immortal flies,
And the worm that never dies.

> And in that Heaven of all their wish,
> There shall be no more land, say fish.
> Rupert Brooke

The last couplet contains examples of some of the basic satirical devices used by Brooke. Its first line is a statement applicable to human beings, and elevation is achieved through the lofty concept (emphasized by the initial capital letter) of 'Heaven'. Its second line parodies a Scriptural quotation ('... and there was no more sea': *Revelations* 21:1) and ends with the bathos of '... say fish'. What other examples of elevation, bathos and Scriptural allusion does the poem contain?

What exactly is Brooke satirizing? Religion generally? Christianity specifically? The mistaken values of some religious believers? Belief in immortality?

Brooke's poem is in the tradition of the 'beast fable' or 'animal fable' in which human beings are represented, often satirically, by animals. Some of the most famous examples of this genre are the fables attributed to Aesop and those written by Jean de la Fontaine. Other well-known examples are Chaucer's 'The Nun's Priest's Tale' and George Orwell's *Animal Farm*. Like so many obsolete literary genres (epic, melodrama, Gothic novel) the beast fable lives on in the cinema, in the form of countless 'cartoons' (e.g. Tom and Jerry).

In such fables the sayings and doings of animals are often described in ironically elevated terms in order to deflate them and the human activities which they represent; Chaucer's cock Chauntecleer, for example, is described as '... royal, as a prince is in his halle'. Attributing human qualities to animals is also a 'distancing' device. We are put (to use another kind of satire as an analogy) in the position of Gulliver, looking down with detached amusement upon the pretentious antics of the Lilliputians: who are in fact ourselves.

Exercise 5

[Americans in Paris]

As the door of Mrs. Pocock's salon was pushed open for him, the next day, well before noon, he was reached by a voice with a charming sound that made him just falter before crossing the threshold. Madame de Vionnet was already on the field, and this gave the drama a quicker pace than he felt it as yet—though his suspense had increased—in the power of any act of his own to do. He had spent the previous evening with all his old friends together; yet he would still have described himself as quite in the dark in respect to a forecast of their influence on his situation. It was strange now, none the less, that in the light of this unexpected note of her presence he felt Madame de Vionnet a part of that situation as she hadn't even yet been. She was alone, he found himself assuming, with Sarah, and there was a bearing in that—somehow beyond his control—on his personal fate. Yet she was only saying something quite easy and independent—the thing she had come, as a good friend of Chad's, on purpose to say. 'There isn't anything at all—? I should be so delighted.'

It was clear enough, when they were there before him, how she had been received. He saw this, as Sarah got up to greet him, from something fairly hectic in Sarah's face. He saw furthermore that they weren't, as had first come to him, alone together; he was at no loss as to the identity of the broad high back presented to him in the embrasure of the window furthest from the door. Waymarsh, whom he had to-day not yet seen, whom he only knew to have left the hotel before him, and who had taken part, the night previous, on Mrs. Pocock's kind invitation, conveyed by Chad, in the entertainment, informal but cordial, promptly offered by that lady—Waymarsh had anticipated him even as Madame de Vionnet had done, and, with his hands in his pockets and his attitude unaffected by Strether's entrance, was looking out, in marked detachment, at the Rue de Rivoli. The latter felt it in the air—it was immense how Waymarsh could mark things—that he had remained deeply dissociated from the overture to their hostess that we have recorded on Madame de Vionnet's side. He had, conspicuously, tact, besides a stiff general view; and this was why he had left Mrs. Pocock to struggle alone. He would outstay the visitor; he would unmistakeably wait; to what had he been doomed for months past but waiting? Therefore she was to feel that she had him in reserve. What support she drew from this was still to be seen, for, although Sarah was vividly bright, she had given herself up for the moment to an ambiguous flushed formalism. She had had to reckon more quickly than she expected; but it concerned her first of all to signify that she was not to be taken unawares. Strether arrived precisely in time for her showing it. 'Oh you're too good; but I don't think I feel quite helpless. I have my brother—and these American friends. And then you know I've been to Paris. I *know* Paris,' said Sally Pocock in a tone that breathed a certain chill on Strether's heart.

'Ah but a woman, in this tiresome place where everything's always changing, a woman of good will,' Madame de Vionnet threw off, 'can always help a woman. I'm sure you "know"—but we know perhaps different things.' She too, visibly, wished to make no mistake; but it was a fear of a different order and more kept out of sight. She smiled in welcome at Strether; she greeted him more familiarly than Mrs. Pocock; she put out her hand to him without moving from her place; and it came to him in the course of a minute and in the oddest way that—yes, positively—she was giving him over to ruin. She was all kindness and ease, but she couldn't help so giving him; she was exquisite, and her being just as she was poured for Sarah a sudden rush of meaning into his own equivocations. How could she know how she was hurting him? She wanted to show as simple and humble— in the degree compatible with operative charm; but it was just this that seemed to put him on her side. She struck him as dressed, as arranged, as prepared infinitely to conciliate—with the very poetry of good taste in her view of the conditions of her early call. She was ready to advise about dressmakers and shops; she held herself wholly at the disposition of Chad's family.

Henry James: from The Ambassadors

Madame de Vionnet is the mistress of Chad Newsome, a young New Englander. Lambert Strether, the central figure in the scene, is a middle-aged widower who hopes to marry Chad's wealthy mother and has come from America to Paris at her request to persuade Chad to give up the liaison and return home. However, Strether has become increasingly sympathetic towards the young couple and their relationship.

At the stage of the novel from which the above extract is taken, Chad's married sister (Sarah Pocock) and other members of his family have just arrived from America with instructions to succeed where Strether has failed. Far from staying discreetly in the background, Madame de Vionnet has made an official call upon Mrs. Pocock, deeply shocking that self-righteously respectable New England matron. The situation is extremely tense: anger and violence threaten to break through the polite social façade, and Waymarsh (another middle-aged American) has turned away in embarrassment. By siding with Madame de Vionnet, Strether will forfeit his own marriage and the comfort and security it offers him.

The occasion is in a sense trivial; but it is genuinely crucial for Strether. James ironically elevates the scene in order to point up its comical absurdity and triviality: much as Pope did with the battle of the young men and women in 'The Rape of the Lock'. Yet the elevation is by no means wholly ironic, for Strether's whole future in fact depends here upon apparently trivial nuances of polite social expression which will indicate to the other characters whether he is going publicly to support Madame de Vionnet or publicly to disown her.

Strether is at once a comic *and* a heroic figure. James's elevated style is simultaneously epic and mock-epic, both ironic and literal at the same time. Describe how James achieves these effects by his use of epic diction, handling of point of view, and control of distance. What are the possible denotations of the word 'embrasure'?

8
Discussion of Passages

Faced with a particular passage of literature to discuss, how should a student set about showing that he is a proficient reader? In this last chapter, after making a few general points, I discuss two poems and two extracts from novels in some detail as examples of how this kind of exercise can be carried out in practice.

In order to show that he is a proficient reader, a student needs to be able to do three things: to perceive the distinctive features of the passage under discussion; to point out these distinctive features to his reader; to explain to his reader what part these distinctive features play in the overall meaning of the passage.

This last ability is crucial. In writing about a piece of literature, there is no point in drawing attention to a distinctive feature and then merely describing it as 'effective'. The student needs to be able to say as clearly as possible *just what effects it has*. He should try to explain as clearly as possible just what the distinctive feature (such as the author's use of elevated diction) contributes to the complex overall statement which the passage makes to its audience.

It is essential to realize that there is no one way of tackling each and every piece of literature. There is no 'correct' all-purpose method. The student could certainly memorize the basic terms and concepts discussed in the previous seven chapters. He should certainly have them in mind as he reads through a passage, and he should certainly use them when he sets out his findings in written form for a tutor or examiner.

But he will reveal a complete misunderstanding of the purpose of this book if he goes through any piece of literature, commenting on its diction, its tone, its pattern, and so on, in some kind of set order, as if these were separable component parts, instead of overlapping aspects or concepts. Which distinctive features of a passage are commented on, and in what order, should always be determined by the passage itself, and by what the student decides are the most important things about it. One might want to draw attention to 'pattern' first of all, in one case, and not even mention it in another.

Although any sort of rigidly schematic approach is to be avoided and in fact deplored, it is still possible to make some helpful general suggestions about the way in which a student might best proceed.

First of all, he should read the passage through slowly at least two or three times in order to get an accurate general impression of its meaning. Next, he should go through it carefully several times, underlining and circling its distinctive features, and trying to work out what effects are achieved by their use. These observations can then be gathered together under headings, in note-form on a piece of paper: e.g. 'Shifting point of view ... Sardonic tone ... Ironic use of clichés ... Humans figuratively likened to animals ...' and so on.

By now, the student should have decided on the main point (or points) which the passage is making. In writing up his observations in the form of a short essay, he should probably *begin* by stating what this main point is (or these main points are), and then proceed to argue his case, citing detailed evidence from the text to support each point he makes. The distinctive features can be brought in one after the other in their order of importance to the particular passage.

For example, if asked to discuss Shelley's 'Ozymandias' in detail, the student might begin: 'Shelly's theme is the transience of earthly power and grandeur. There is no trace of nostalgia in his treatment of this theme. On the contrary, he invents a desolate scene and an unpleasantly vainglorious tyrant in order to emphasize the sheer folly of human self-satisfaction about the durability of earthly achievements. Shelley expresses his adverse judgement of the representative figure of Ozymandias through different kinds of irony ...' The student might then describe the different kinds of irony employed. Having done this, he might go on to talk about the parts played in the overall meaning of the poem by the adverse terms used in connection with Ozymandias (e.g. 'sneer'), the contrasts between words such as 'colossal' and 'level', and the functions of the setting generally. Something might be said in conclusion about Shelley's exceptionally tight control of the sonnet form. Having established one point convincingly, the student should always move on to the next, avoiding repetition.

One way of making the distinctive features of a piece of writing more obvious, if the student has time, is to try to match it against another piece which is concerned with the same theme or a similar subject-matter. It would be easy to pair 'Ozymandias', for example, with one of the countless poems which employ the *'ubi sunt* theme' (see 'Additional Terms').

To indicate the advantages of this method, I have used it myself in the discussions of particular passages which follow. William Blake's poem 'London' is compared and contrasted with Wordsworth's 'Composed upon Westminster Bridge', and an extract from Dickens's *Our*

Mutual Friend is compared and contrasted with one from George Eliot's *Middlemarch.*

(i) Wordsworth and Blake

Composed upon Westminster Bridge

Earth has not anything to show more fair:
Dull would he be of soul who could pass by
A sight so touching in its majesty:
This City now doth, like a garment, wear
The beauty of the morning; silent, bare,
Ships, towers, domes, theatres, and temples lie
Open unto the fields, and to the sky;
All bright and glittering in the smokeless air.
Never did sun more beautifully steep
In his first splendour, valley, rock, or hill;
Ne'er saw I, never felt, a calm so deep!
The river glideth at his own sweet will:
Dear God! the very houses seem asleep;
And all that mighty heart is lying still!

London

I wander thro' each charter'd street,
Near where the charter'd Thames does flow,
And mark in every face I meet
Marks of weakness, marks of woe.

In every cry of every Man,
In every Infant's cry of fear,
In every voice, in every ban,
The mind-forg'd manacles I hear.

How the Chimney-sweeper's cry
Every black'ning Church appalls;
And the hapless Soldier's sigh
Runs in blood down Palace walls.

But most thro' midnight streets I hear
How the youthful Harlot's curse
Blasts the new born Infant's tear,
And blights with plagues the Marriage hearse.

Both poems are about London, and both make use of hyperbole, or over-statement. For Wordsworth, the entire earth contains *nothing* fairer than London in the early morning, and the word 'never' is used three times to stress the uniqueness of its beauty. For Blake, the 'mind-forged manacles' are detectable in '*every* voice' and '*every* ban', and the word 'every' is used no less than seven times in order to stress their all-pervading influence. Although both poems are highly evaluative, they express attitudes which are completely opposed to each other: Wordsworth strongly approves of the city as a place of natural beauty, while Blake equally strongly disapproves of it as unnatural and diseased.

Each poet singles out particular aspects of his subject-matter and emphasizes these to the exclusion of everything else, at the same time expressing attitudes towards them by means of evaluative diction and figurative language. Wordsworth presents the city mainly in terms of its buildings (there are no people in his poem), and uses the following words in connection with it: 'fair', 'beauty', 'bright', 'glittering', 'beautifully', 'sweet'. These terms beautify the city, while the elevating words 'majesty', 'splendour' and 'mighty' dignify and ennoble it. Wordsworth also *personifies* both the forces of Nature and the aspects of the city which he is describing: the sun steeps the city 'in *his* ... splendour', while the river glides 'at *his* own sweet will'; the city, on the other hand, possesses 'majesty'; it 'wears' the beauty of the morning 'like a garment'; it is the nation's 'mighty heart'; its buildings are 'bare', and its houses 'seem asleep'. The effect of these personifications is to present the city, not as something cut off from Nature, but as a living part of the life of Nature itself.

The beauty of the city, for Wordsworth, is above all the beauty of tranquillity; this is made particularly apparent in line 11, where approval for the uniquely 'deep' 'calm' is emphasized by two hyperbolic 'never's and an exclamation-mark. Wordsworth uses no forceful or energetic verbs which would destroy the impression of this soothing calm: 'wear', 'lie', 'steep', 'glideth' and 'lying' are all verbs which denote little if any activity, and certainly no noise.

Compared with Wordsworth's London, Blake's is a noisy and populous place, full of cries, voices, sighs, curses, and the people who utter them. Indeed, the city is presented largely in terms of certain of its inhabitants: infants, chimney-sweeps, soldiers and harlots. We need to know, here, that chimney-sweeps in Blake's day were little boys who climbed up chimneys to dislodge the soot: a dangerous and dehumanizing job which often caused cancer.

Knowing this, we can see that these inhabitants of Blake's London are victims of economic exploitation, the cast-off soldier no less than the climbing-boy and the child-prostitute. Their lives are not only warped by society, but diseased. The soldier is consumptive, and the venereal disease passed on by the youthful harlot infects both new-born children and the partners of marriages: it 'blasts' and 'blights' marriages (both words denote the effects of destructive diseases) with its 'plagues'.

Meanwhile the Church and the State ('Palace'), which should be helping these unfortunates, remain aloof and indifferent. According to Blake, these unnatural perversions of human society and natural life are all caused by 'mind-forged manacles': the narrow and inflexible attitudes to our fellow-men which are brought about by thinking of them in terms of purely rational (even economic) calculation, instead of feeling for them with Christian love. In the reference to 'Palace walls' there may be a hint that the wealthy and the powerful will shortly, like Belshazzar, be overthrown (see the Old Testament *Book of Daniel*: V, v).

'Mind-forged manacles' is an example of Blake's ability to create new and startling figures of speech which have the effect of putting abstract issues into tangible and pictorial form. Other examples of this are the soldier's sigh, which 'runs in blood' down the walls of a palace, and the 'marriage hearse' which ends the poem. A sigh cannot literally 'run in blood' down a palace-wall, of course; but the figure of speech translates into physical terms both the soldier's anguish which gives rise to the sigh, and the stony indifference of the State authorities. 'Marriage hearse' is even more startling. The sort of phrase we would expect Blake to use is 'marriage-*bed*', with all its acquired connotations of married love and fertility. But marriage, because of venereal disease, has become a hearse, something which carries one to the graveyard, a means to death and destruction instead of a means to the renewal of life.

Two other distinctive features of Blake's manner of writing deserve particular attention: the irony and compression which he achieves by the use of ambiguous words and phrases, and his use of parallelisms.

A number of Blake's words and phrases are used in two or more senses at the same time. Such words are 'charter'd', 'mark(s)', 'cry', 'church', 'blackening', 'appalls', 'curse', and 'blasts'. 'Chartered' means 'licensed', and in two opposed senses of that word: 'controlled by those who grant and receive licences', and, virtually, 'licentious';* Blake implies that the streets and the river which should be free to

* According to *The Oxford English Dictionary* Blake is here using 'chartered' as in Shakespeare's 'a chartered libertine' (*Henry V*). In this sense it means 'licensed' or 'freely immoral'. For 'licence' denoting 'excessive freedom' and connoting 'lawless immorality', cf. Milton's famous distinction: 'Licence they mean when they cry liberty.'

all citizens are controlled and restricted by financial interests, and, ironically, that the only 'freedom' is that of sexual immorality. 'Mark' as a verb means 'observe' or 'notice'; 'marks of weakness' are visible *indications* of weakness, while 'marks of woe' are visible *traces* of woe. The chimney-sweeper's cry is both his street-cry of 'Sweep! Sweep!' and his cry of misery. The churches are both physical buildings and, collectively, the Church as a Christian institution. They are 'blackening' in the sense of 'becoming covered with soot' and also in the sense of 'losing their spiritual purity'. Ironically, the cry of the sweep does 'appall' them in one way, by figuratively covering them with a pall of soot; but it is the sweep's wretchedness which should *morally* appal the Church as an institution, and it takes no notice of him. The youthful harlot's 'curse / Blasts the new-born infant's tear' in two ways: she curses the sound of the child's crying with an oath ('*Blast* that yelling brat!'); and the 'curse' of her venereal disease has already physically infected and tainted the purity of a new-born baby's tears.

The effect of these ambiguities is to build up a complex and often ironical presentation of London's degraded condition, and of the causes of its degradation. In particular, they suggest that the same causes and the same effects permeate and corrupt every aspect of life.

Finally, it should be pointed out that Blake makes considerable use of parallelisms, such as 'Marks of weakness, marks of woe'; 'In every cry of every man, / In every infant's cry of fear'; 'the chimney-sweeper's cry' ... 'the hapless soldier's sigh' ... 'the youthful harlot's curse'. These patterns, intensified by the heavily-stressed rhyming words, emphasize the similarities between the conditions of life of the representative types of people portrayed. By stressing what their conditions have in common, Blake can more convincingly argue that woes so identical must have an identical cause; his complex and systematizing mind sees all human misery as the product of the 'mind-forged manacles'.

In concluding this comparison, something should be said about the degree of patterning in Wordsworth's sonnet. The poem consists of only two sentences, each entirely occupying the first eight lines (the 'octave') and the last six lines (the 'sestet') respectively.

Although the sonnet form demands great technical expertise from the writer, Wordsworth does not (except perhaps for the triple repetition of 'never') create symmetrical patterns of syntax which would draw attention to his own organizing presence and ingenuity. Rather, by running-on four of the fourteen lines and by heavily punctuating seven of them internally (especially lines 6 and 13), he avoids any suggestion of literary contrivance, producing instead the impression that the poem is being spoken out aloud at the actual moment of heightened emotion. The effect produced is that of impassioned, elevated, grave yet informal speech.

(ii) George Eliot and Charles Dickens

When Mr. Brooke presented himself on the balcony, the cheers were quite loud enough to counterbalance the yells, groans, brayings, and other expressions of adverse theory, which were so moderate that Mr. Standish (decidedly an old bird) observed in the ear next to him, 'This looks dangerous, by God! Hawley has got some deeper plan than this.' Still, the cheers were exhilarating, and no candidate could look more amiable than Mr. Brooke, with the memorandum in his breast-pocket, his left hand on the rail of the balcony, and his right trifling with his eye-glass. The striking points in his appearance were his buff waistcoat, short-clipped blond hair, and neutral physiognomy. He began with some confidence.

'Gentlemen—Electors of Middlemarch!'

This was so much the right thing that a little pause after it seemed natural.

'I'm uncommonly glad to be here—I was never so proud and happy in my life— never so happy, you know.'

This was a bold figure of speech, but not exactly the right thing; for, unhappily, the pat opening had slipped away—even couplets from Pope may be but 'fallings from us, vanishings,' when fear clutches us, and a glass of sherry is hurrying like smoke among our ideas. Ladislaw, who stood at the window behind the speaker, thought, 'It's all up now. The only chance is that since the best thing won't always do floundering may answer for once.' Mr. Brooke, meanwhile, having lost other clues, fell back on himself and his qualifications—always an appropriate graceful subject for a candidate.

'I am a close neighbour of yours, my good friends—you've known me on the bench a good while—I've always gone a good deal into public questions— machinery, now, and machine-breaking—you're many of you concerned with machinery, and I've been going into that lately. It won't do, you know, breaking machines: everything must go on—trade, manufactures, commerce, interchange of staples—that kind of thing—since Adam Smith, that must go on. We must look all over the globe:—"Observation with extensive view," must look everywhere, "from China to Peru," as somebody says—Johnson, I think, "The Rambler," you know. That is what I have done up to a certain point—not as far as Peru; but I've not always stayed at home—I saw it wouldn't do. I've been in the Levant, where some of your Middlemarch goods go—and then, again, in the Baltic. The Baltic, now.'

Plying among his recollections in this way, Mr. Brooke might have got along, easily to himself, and would have come back from the remotest seas without trouble; but a diabolical procedure had been set up by the enemy. At one and the same moment there had risen above the shoulders of the crowd, nearly opposite Mr. Brooke, and within ten yards of him, the effigy of himself; buff-coloured waist-coat, eye-glass, and neutral physiognomy, painted on rag; and there had arisen apparently in the air, like the note of the cuckoo, a parrot-like, Punch-voiced echo of his words. Everybody looked up at the open windows in the houses at the opposite angles of the converging streets; but they were either blank, or filled by laugh-ing listeners. The most innocent echo has an impish mockery in it when it follows a gravely persistent speaker, and this echo was not at all innocent; if it did not follow with the precision of a natural echo, it had a wicked choice of the words it overtook. By the time it said, "The Baltic, now," the laugh which had been running through the audience became a general shout, and but for the sobering effects of party and that great public cause which the entanglement of things had identified with "Brooke of Tipton," the laugh might have caught his committee. Mr. Bulstrode asked, reprehensively, what the new police was doing; but a voice could not well be collared, and an attack on the effigy of the candidate would have been too equivocal since Hawley probably meant it to be pelted.

Mr. Brooke himself was not in a position to be quickly conscious of anything except a general slipping away of ideas within himself: he had even a little singing in the ears, and he was the only person who had not yet taken distinct account of the echo or discerned the image of himself. Few things hold the perceptions more thoroughly captive than anxiety about what we have got to say. Mr. Brooke heard the laughter; but he had expected some Tory efforts at disturbance, and he was at this moment additionally excited by the tickling, stinging sense that his lost exordium was coming back to fetch him from the Baltic.

George Eliot: from *Middlemarch*

When the time comes for Veneering to deliver a neat and appropriate stammer to the men of Pocket-Breaches, only Podsnap and Twemlow accompany him by railway to that sequestered spot. The legal gentleman is at the Pocket-Breaches Branch Station, with an open carriage with a printed bill, 'Veneering for ever!' stuck upon it, as if it were a wall; and they gloriously proceed, amidst the grins of the populace, to a feeble little town hall on crutches, with some onions and bootlaces under it, which the legal gentleman says are a Market; and from the front window of that edifice Veneering speaks to the listening earth. In the moment of his taking his hat off, Podsnap, as per agreement made with Mrs. Veneering, telegraphs to that wife and mother, 'He's up.'

Veneering loses his way in the usual No Thoroughfares of speech, and Podsnap and Twemlow say 'Hear hear!' and sometimes, when he can't by any means back himself out of some very unlucky No Thoroughfare, 'He-a-a-r He-a-a-r!' with an air of facetious conviction, as if the ingenuity of the thing gave them a sensation of exquisite pleasure. But Veneering makes two remarkably good points; so good, that they are supposed to have been suggested to him by the legal gentleman in Britannia's confidence, while briefly conferring on the stairs.

Point the first is this. Veneering institutes an original comparison between the country and a ship; pointedly calling the ship, the Vessel of the State, and the Minister the Man at the Helm. Veneering's object is to let Pocket-Breaches know that his friend on his right (Podsnap) is a man of wealth. Consequently says he, 'And, gentleman, when the timbers of the Vessel of the State are unsound and the Man at the Helm is unskilful, would those great Marine Insurers, who rank among our world-famed merchant-princes—would they insure her, gentlemen? Would they underwrite her? Would they incur a risk in her? Would they have confidence in her? Why, gentleman, if I appealed to my honourable friend upon my right, himself among the greatest and most respected of that great and much respected class, he would answer No!'

Point the second is this. The telling fact that Twemlow is related to Lord Snigsworth, must be let off. Veneering supposes a state of public affairs that probably never could by any possibility exist (though this is not quite certain, in consequence of his picture being unintelligible to himself, and everybody else), and thus proceeds. 'Why, gentlemen, if I were to indicate such a programme to any class of society, I say it would be received with derision, would be pointed at by the finger of scorn. If I indicated such a programme to any worthy and intelligent tradesman of your town—nay, I will here be personal, and say Our town—what would he reply? He would reply, "Away with it!" That's what *he* would reply, gentlemen. In his honest indignation he would reply, "Away with it!" But suppose I mounted higher in the social scale. Suppose I drew my arm through the arm of my respected friend upon my left, and, walking with him through the ancestral woods of his family, and under the spreading beeches of Snigsworthy Park, approached the noble hall, crossed the courtyard, entered by the door, went up the staircase, and, passing from room to room, found myself at last in the august presence of my friend's near kinsman, Lord Snigsworth. And suppose I said to that venerable earl, "My Lord, I am here before your lordship, presented by your lordship's near kinsman, my friend upon my left, to indicate that programme;" what would his lordship answer? Why, he would answer, "Away with it!" That's what he would answer, gentlemen. "Away with it!" Unconsciously using, in his exalted sphere, the exact language of the worthy and intelligent tradesmen of our town, the near and dear kinsman of my friend upon my left would answer in his wrath, "Away with it!" '

Veneering finishes with this last success, and Mr. Podsnap telegraphs to Mrs. Veneering, 'He's down.'

Then dinner is had at the Hotel with the legal gentleman, and then there are in due succession, nomination and declaration. Finally Mr. Podsnap telegraphs to Mrs. Veneering, 'We have brought him in.'

Charles Dickens: from *Our Mutual Friend*

Both passages describe election meetings for parliamentary candidates in a humorous manner, and both (as we shall see) use much the same kinds of ironic manœuvre. Dickens writes as a political and social reformer; his genially destructive political satire is directed against the tradition of 'Veneering for ever', or the pretence of democracy without the reality (a 'veneer' being a thin sheet of superior material which is used to hide inferior material). George Eliot writes as a moral reformer who is concerned to enlarge our sympathies and understanding by demonstrating the complex ironies of life, or what she calls 'the entanglement of things'.

Both authors involve their characters in ironic situations, give ironic impersonations of them, and make ironic comments about them and about other topics. Mr. Brooke's ironic situation is the classic one of *unawareness*, and it is doubly ironic because what he cannot see is actually a parody of himself: 'he was the *only* person who had not yet taken distinct account of the echo or discerned the image of himself'. The irony of Mr. Veneering's situation is not directed against him personally, but against a political abuse of the period prior to 1832: Pocket-Breaches is a 'pocket borough', in which there is no candidate to oppose him. The result of the election is a foregone conclusion, Mr. Veneering's speech is a formality and a sham, and the mechanical nature of the process by which he becomes an M.P. is emphasized by Mr. Podsnap's ludicrously unnecessary series of snappy telegrams: 'He's up.' ... 'He's down.' ... 'We have brought him in.' Dickens's use of the present tense throughout the passage also has the effect of conveying the speed and inevitability of the process, rather in the manner of a present-day racing commentator.

Dickens's ironic impersonation of Mr. Veneering's speech is also not intended to satirize him personally, but spurious political rhetoric generally. This is suggested by the unusually large number of obvious clichés with which he equips his character: 'the finger of scorn', 'august presence', 'honest indignation', and so on. Dickens also arranges for each part of Veneering's grotesque speech to culminate, not in a splendidly oratorical conclusion, but in an utterly deflating bathos: the extremely banal 'No!' at the end of the first part, and the equally banal 'Away with it!' at the end of the second part.

George Eliot's ironic impersonation of Mr. Brooke's election address serves no such general purpose. She is concerned to present him as an individual character, a well-meaning but hopelessly incompetent amateur who stands not the slightest chance against the opposition and their 'diabolical procedure'. Mr. Brooke, unknown to himself, reveals both his incompetence and his gentlemanly semi-ignorance. There is a double irony in his mis-attributing the quotation from Dr. Johnson to 'The Rambler', for it is of course Mr. Brooke who is the 'rambler' in his disconnected method of speaking, and the quotation really comes (with an ironic appropriateness of which he is entirely unaware) from Johnson's 'The Vanity of Human Wishes'.

Both authors make a large number of ironic comments, often of a deflationary kind. George Eliot mockingly describes the sub-human 'yells, groans, brayings' of the crowd as 'expressions of adverse *theory*', as if they were the product of rational and high-minded political philosophizing. Mr. Brooke's second banal remark is described as 'a bold figure of speech', and the 'most striking points' in his appearance are those of a complete nonentity. Again, he is described as 'plying' among his recollections: the term, which has to do with shipping, is appropriate to his talk about the Baltic and the Levant; insofar as it connotes purposeful regularity, however, it is a wildly inappropriate word to use in connection with his disordered ramblings.

Dickens's ironic comments are equally deflating, but considerably less subtle, relying either on obvious bathos or on the implying of meanings which are quite simply the opposites of the ones stated. Bathos is being employed when we are told that Mr. Veneering is to 'deliver', not a speech, but a 'stammer', and when we are told that the four men 'gloriously proceed ... to a feeble little town hall on crutches'. The following comments mean the *exact* opposite of what they appear to state: Mr. Veneering 'makes two remarkably good points' (i.e. remarkably *bad* points); he 'institutes an original comparison' (i.e. an utterly *hackneyed* one); he finishes 'with this last success' (i.e. this last dismal *failure*). Dickens, unlike George Eliot, also makes ironic use of clichés, not only in his ironic impersonation of Mr. Veneering, but in his own comments as narrator: Pocket-Breaches is 'that sequestered spot'; Mrs. Podsnap is 'that wife and mother'; the electorate of Pocket-Breaches are the entire 'listening earth'. The effect here is to draw attention to the hypocrisy which underlies the use of such clichés.

In their use of ironic manœuvres, Eliot and Dickens might be said to be broadly similar to each other. They are vastly different from each other, however, in their use of intrusive authorial comments, in the distance which they create between the reader and their characters, and in their handling of narrative point of view.

Dickens makes three comments directly to the reader: he tells us that 'Veneering's object is to let Pocket-Breaches know that his friend ... is a man of wealth', that 'The telling fact that Twemlow is related to Lord Snigsworth, must be let off', and that Veneering's 'picture' is unintelligible to himself and to everybody else. These are explanatory comments, designed to guide the reader through the confusions of Veneering's speech, and to make quite sure that he appreciates each bathos when it eventually arrives.

Two of George Eliot's 'intrusive' comments are characteristically addressed to *us* as readers, and include herself as author: '... even couplets from Pope may be but "fallings from *us*, vanishings,"* when fear clutches *us*, and a glass of sherry is hurrying like smoke among *our* ideas'; 'Few things hold the perceptions more thoroughly captive than anxiety about what *we* have got to say'. Her other intrusive comment

* The quotation is from Wordsworth's 'Ode: Intimations of Immortality', and the two lines which follow it describe the unfortunate Mr. Brooke's situation exactly: 'Blank misgivings of a Creature/Moving about in worlds not realised'.

is also a generalization: 'The most innocent echo has an impish mockery about it when it follows a gravely persistent speaker ...'. These generalizations have the important effect of decreasing the distance between ourselves and Mr. Brooke, and enlisting sympathy for him. George Eliot reminds us that Mr. Brooke is not unique in his state of comical confusion, but every bit as human as we are and as she is. Indeed, we may begin to discover rather uneasily, towards the end of the extract, that the author has begun to turn our laughter at Mr. Brooke back upon ourselves.

There is not the slightest hint of sympathy for Veneering, Podsnap and Twemlow: Dickens's distance from his characters is absolute. They are farcical buffoons, presented entirely from the outside, with nothing to suggest that they have the inner fears, doubts and hesitations common to all men. Their names are labels which invite us to regard them as comic *types*, to be thought of only in terms of their outward behaviour and appearance. A man with a name like 'Veneering' can only be an oily rascal. 'Podsnap' bespeaks a pompous dogmatist, while 'Twemlow' is both timid and effete ('tremolo', spoken with a lisp). 'The legal gentleman' is just that, three times, and is endowed with no human characteristics whatsoever. Dickens writes in the comic tradition of Fielding and Ben Jonson, with their 'humour' characters (i.e. highly simplified character types) such as Lady Booby, and Sir Epicure Mammon.

George Eliot, on the other hand, further invites us to identify and sympathize with Mr. Brooke by occasionally presenting him from the inside. The sentence beginning 'This was so much the right thing ...' is what Mr Brooke thinks to himself, and is so breathtakingly naïve that our amusement must be tempered with pity. The sentence about Pope, already commented upon, conveys Mr. Brooke's inner fear and confusion to the reader, while most of the last paragraph of the extract aims to convey to the reader just what it feels like to *be* Mr. Brooke: 'slipping away of ideas *within* himself ... singing *in* the ears ... tickling, stinging *sense*'.

George Eliot also shifts her narrative point of view to include Ladislaw's inner thoughts ('It's all up now ...'), the whispered comment of Mr. Standish, and Mr. Bulstrode's question about the police. Her narrative techniques, much more complex on this occasion than those of Dickens, build up a much more complicated representation of human life, in which we are simultaneously aware of what a number of characters are doing, saying and thinking, *and* being asked to evaluate the situation in terms of our own experience. Dickens insists upon a simple moral judgement from the reader, while George Eliot is fully determined to deny him that luxury. She also makes more demands upon the reader's education than does Dickens in her allusions (Adam Smith, Pope, Wordsworth, Dr. Johnson) and in her diction ('reprehensively', 'equivocal', 'exordium').

To sum up, then: Dickens writes in the grand tradition of farcical exaggeration. He employs fairly obvious and repetitious ironies, a restricted narrative technique, highly simplified and exaggerated characters, together with a ludicrous situation, to produce a comically simple political satire. George Eliot employs less obvious and more varied ironies, a highly flexible narrative technique, more realistically complex characters, and a more realistically complex situation. The combined effect of these is to encourage us to view ourselves and others with a compassionate irony, in which sympathy and comic detachment are equally blended.

*   *   *

One thing which Dickens and George Eliot have in common is that they both aim, as Sir Philip Sidney put it, 'to teach and delight'. And they have this in common, not only with each other, but with most of the other authors who have been touched upon in this book.

9
Additional Terms

The following terms, about twenty in all, have been chosen because they are particularly useful to students. Most of them refer to poetry, and in particular to aspects of poetry which have been fixed and formalized by tradition: to traditional verse-forms such as the heroic couplet and the sonnet, to traditional themes or topics such as the *carpe diem* theme and the *ubi sunt* theme, and to traditional 'kinds' of poem such as the elegy and the ode.

Poets, in particular, often work within certain fixed conventions, and the reader can grasp the distinctive features of a particular poem more easily if he is able to identify any conventions or traditions which the poem employs, and can mentally compare the author's use of these with the ways in which they have been employed by other writers. Knowledge of these conventions and traditions, in short, provides us with a basis for comparisons which throw into relief the particular qualities of a particular poem.

The entries which follow are not intended to do much more than bring certain terms to the reader's attention and very briefly to indicate their importance. Students are recommended to read the more detailed and comprehensive entries provided in a glossary of literary terms such as that by M. H. Abrams (see 'Further Reading').

*   *   *

allusions: Authors often make allusions, or references, to notable figures and incidents from the past, and to notable written and artistic works. The passages discussed in this book, though chosen for other reasons, turn out to be full of allusions: to the Bible (Blake, Faulkner, Pope), to classical mythology (Fielding, Joyce, Yeats), and to other works of literature (George Eliot, T. S. Eliot).

Allusions of this kind often play an extremely important part in the overall meaning of a passage of writing. Indeed, a brief allusion may well be the single most important feature of a particular passage, in the sense that everything else in the passage relates to it and depends upon it. It is clearly essential for us to make sure that we understand every allusion in a passage which we are reading. Most allusions can be quickly looked up in a dictionary of quotations, and a student should certainly buy his own copy of such a dictionary as that edited by J. M. and M. J. Cohen (see 'Further Reading').

ambiguity: An ambiguity is an ambiguous word or expression: one which means more than one thing at a time. Ambiguities can be accidental, as when we fail to make our meaning clear in speech or in writing; or they can be used *deliberately* to achieve certain effects. Deliberate ambiguities abound in everyday discourse, particularly in jokes, puns and riddles; these often depend on quite complex verbal ambiguities whose effects we would probably find hard to explain, but which we are capable of responding to with lightning speed. The anonymous poem 'Willie's Epitaph' ends with two such ambiguities:

> Little Willie from his mirror
> Licked the mercury right off,
> Thinking, in his childish error,
> It would cure the whooping cough.
> At the funeral his mother
> Smartly said to Mrs. Brown:
> ' 'Twas a chilly day for Willie
> When the mercury went down'.

Literary writers often make deliberate use of ambiguous words and expressions, as may be seen from the comments made in previous chapters on writings by Wilde, Shelley, and Blake. Here, as another example, are the famous last lines of Sir John Denham's poem 'Cooper's Hill':

> O could I flow like thee, and make thy stream
> My great example, as it is my theme!
> Though deep, yet clear, though gentle, yet not dull,
> Strong without rage, without o'er-flowing full.

In these lines, which make considerable use of parallel and antithesis, Denham is addressing the River Thames: that is his 'theme'. He also wishes the Thames to be his 'example' or model, and in two senses: he wishes that his own life and personality could possess the qualities that he attributes to the river; and also that his own poetry could possess them. Most of Denham's words and phrases then, are to be read in three senses simultaneously, as applying to the river, to his life, and to his poetry. I.e. the Thames as a body of water is deep yet clear; Denham wishes to be a serious-minded person ('deep') yet open and frank to others ('clear'); he wishes his poetry to be profound ('deep') yet easily understood ('clear').

We should always be on the alert for such ambiguities in a passage of literary writing, and having detected them should be prepared if necessary to try to explain them and their effects. This is far from easy. However, a *good* dictionary such as *The American College Dictionary*

(Random House) is invaluable for helping one decide which of a word's particular connotations are being used in one of these complex situations.

blank verse: The most commonly used verse form in English, consisting of unrhymed lines of ten syllables each. These ten syllables are thought of in theoretical terms as being divided into five iambic feet, each consisting of an unstressed followed by a stressed syllable, as in the word '*avoid*': hence the term 'iambic pentameter'.

Most blank verse of any quality contains no regular iambic pentameters whatsoever: see for example the extract from Wordsworth's 'Michael' reproduced in Chapter 6 ('Pattern'). There is consequently little if any point in a student's making a detailed metrical analysis of a passage of blank verse (or indeed of any other form of verse, for that matter). However, he should certainly be able to recognize when a poet is using blank verse, and whether he is using it in a regular, formal and possibly monotonous way, end-stopping nearly every line, or whether he is using it so fluently and flexibly that the result is very close to colloquial English speech.

carpe diem: This Latin phrase meaning 'seize the day' comes from a famous ode by Horace which begins 'Seize today, and put as little trust as you can in the morrow'. So many poems have been written in this vein, emphasizing the shortness of life and the fleetingness of pleasure, that taken together they constitute a minor tradition of some importance. When we encounter such poems as Marvell's 'To His Coy Mistress' and Henry King's 'Sic Vita' ('Such is Life') we should be able to recognize that they belong to this tradition, and should be able mentally to compare and contrast them with other examples.

cliché: An expression, often a figure of speech or a quotation, which has lost its force through repetition: e.g. 'to leave no stone unturned', 'alternative lifestyles', 'fresh fields and pastures new' (the usually misquoted last line from Milton's 'Lycidas'). Clichés abound in everyday life: in conversation, in newspaper editorials, in political speeches, and of course in the descriptive passages, dialogue and situations of run-of-the-mill fiction, plays, films and television-serials. Clichés are also therefore the essential raw material out of which ironic impersonators and parodists from James Joyce to Barry Humphries fashion their critiques of contemporary life and letters.

It is clearly essential for us (a) to be able to recognize a cliché, and (b) to be able to detect whether it is being used *innocently* or *ironically*.

Two books in particular can be recommended to anyone who wishes to sharpen his eye for clichés: Eric Partridge's *A Dictionary of Clichés* (1940) and James Joyce's *Ulysses*, which amongst other things is a comic anthology of most of the journalistic and literary clichés known to Western man (e.g. 'But how to get there was the rub. For the nonce he was rather nonplussed but inasmuch as the duty plainly devolved upon him to take some measures on the subject he pondered suitable ways and means during which Stephen repeatedly yawned.')

conceit: A particularly striking figure of comparison whose ingenuity draws attention both to itself and to the skill of the author who contrived it. In the sacred and secular love-poems of such seriously witty seventeenth-century 'Metaphysical' poets as John Donne and George Herbert, conceits often have the effect of distancing the passionate feelings expressed.

couplet: In poetry, two successive lines (usually of the same length) which rhyme with each other. The commonest forms are the heroic couplet (two rhyming ten-syllable lines) and the octosyllabic couplet (two rhyming eight-syllables lines). Pope's satirical 'portrait' of Lord Hervey (Chapter 5) and Goldsmith's *The Deserted Village* (Chapter 6) are written in heroic couplets. Marvell's 'To His Coy Mistress' is written in octosyllabic couplets, thus:

> But at my back I always hear
> Time's wingèd chariot hurrying near ...

Couplets make possible a high degree of patterning. As with blank verse, we need to be able to recognize when this form is being used in a regular, formal and possibly monotonous way, or whether the poet uses run-on lines and internally punctuated lines to achieve more varied and informal effects. In the hands of Pope, for example, the heroic couplet can range from the comparatively regular and formal to the comparatively irregular and informal:

> Here the bright crocus and blue violet glow;
> Here western winds on breathing roses blow.
> *(Pastorals:* 'Spring')

> 'Shut, shut the door, good John!' fatigued, I said,
> 'Tie up the knocker, say I'm sick, I'm dead.'
> ('Epistle to Dr. Arbuthnot')

elegy: A poem of lament for the death of a particular person; or, like Gray's 'Elegy Written in a Country Churchyard', a meditative poem. Like epic poems (see Chapter 7) and odes, elegies are formal and ceremonial poems which use elevated diction to dignify their subject-matter.

epigram: An ingeniously compact and often witty statement in either verse or prose. E.g. 'A hen is only an egg's way of making another egg' (Samuel Butler); 'Experience is the name every one gives to their mistakes' (Oscar Wilde); 'For fools rush in where angels fear to tread' (Pope). Epigrams, like conceits, tend to draw attention to the controlling and directing presence of their authors.

euphemism: A word or phrase with dignified connotations which is used in place of one having connotations regarded as undignified or offensive. E.g. 'Senior Citizen' for 'old-age pensioner'; 'New Australian' for 'migrant'; 'retrenchment' for 'sacking'; 'rodent operator' for 'rat-catcher'; 'lower back' for 'buttocks'; 'comfort station' for 'lavatory', 'economically underprivileged' for 'poor'.

Euphemisms are extremely interesting everyday examples of elevated diction.

free verse or **vers libre**: Unrhymed verse written in lines of irregular length, and a hallmark of self-consciously 'modern' poetry since the Imagist movement of 1911 or thereabouts (see T. E. Hulme's poem 'Autumn', Chapter 2).

Free verse, even more than the extremely colloquial and irregular blank verse of Wordsworth's 'Michael', is an extreme example of a low degree of patterning in verse. In such poems as D. H. Lawrence's 'Snake' it is used in order to present a particular moment in all its uniqueness, instead of incorporating the experience into some logical and systematic way of looking at life in general.

lyric: A short poem whose main concern is to express the speaker's heightened state of mind and, especially, feeling (e.g. Wordsworth's 'Composed Upon Westminster Bridge').

occasional poem: A poem written to commemorate a particular event or *occasion* of some significance, either personal (the marriage of a friend, perhaps) or public (Independence Day). Occasional poems are usually formal and elevated.

octave: see 'sonnet'.

ode: An ode is a serious lyric poem of some length, written in praise of a person or a group of people, or in praise or contemplation of such things as ideas and institutions. E.g. Keats's 'Ode to a Nightingale'; Wordsworth's 'Ode to Duty'. A 'national anthem' such as 'Advance

Australia Fair' is a short sung ode in praise of a particular nation. Odes, like epics and elegies, are formal and ceremonial poems which use elevated diction to dignify their subject-matter.

pastoral: The pastoral tradition in literature is both widespread and persistent, based as it is upon the nostalgic yearning of urban sophisticates for an alleged Golden Age of rural simplicity and innocence. Virgil's *Eclogues*, based upon the poems of Theocritus, provided the example for innumerable works of literature, ranging from Shakespeare's *As You Like It* to Pope's *Pastorals*, which presented an idealized world of shepherds and country folk. The pastoral elegy, such as Milton's 'Lycidas', is an extremely conventionalized and elevated poem which depicts the mourner and his dead friend as shepherds.

The pastoral tradition lives on vigorously in many forms, such as the numerous American films and television-serials whose main concern is to depict the untainted innocence and robust simplicity of frontier society.

pentameter: see 'blank verse'.

quatrain: A verse stanza of four lines, usually with alternate rhymes. As with 'couplets', we should be able to recognize whether a poet's quatrains are neat and regular, or whether irregularities are introduced by means of run-on lines and internally punctuated lines.

sestet: see 'sonnet'.

sonnet: A poem, often a lyric poem, consisting of fourteen ten-syllable lines with a complex rhyming pattern. The Petrarchan sonnet divides into two main parts: the octave, or first eight lines; and the sestet, or last six lines. The octave often describes a specific situation which is generalized upon in the sestet. The English (or Shakespearian) sonnet consists of three quatrains followed by a concluding couplet, often of an epigrammatic kind.

We need to be able to recognize which of these two main kinds of sonnet is being used, so that we can judge the extent to which a basic pattern is being adhered to or departed from. As with other fixed forms such as 'couplets' and 'quatrains', sonnets may be neat, regular, controlled and therefore distanced, or they may use run-on lines and internally punctuated lines to achieve the impression of passionate speech, as in Yeats's 'Leda and the Swan' (Chapter 1) and Wordsworth's 'Composed Upon Westminster Bridge' (Chapter 8).

stanza: A group of lines of verse, such as a 'quatrain', which is repeated according to a fixed pattern to form the units of a poem.

ubi sunt: This Latin phrase meaning 'Where are ...?' is used to denote the theme or topic of countless poems which express regret for a vanished past, and which, like '*carpe diem*' poems, draw attention to the fleetingness of time.

W. B. Henley's 'Ballade of Dead Actors' is an excellent example of an '*ubi sunt*' poem; here is its first stanza:

> Where are the passions they essayed,
> And where the tears they made to flow?
> Where the wild humours they portrayed
> For laughing worlds to see and know?
> Othello's wrath and Juliet's woe?
> Sir Peter's whims and Timon's gall?
> And Millamant and Romeo?
> Into the night go one and all.

10
Further Reading

Reference Books

As mentioned earlier, the student needs a dictionary which lists the many different denotations of words and describes their connotations in detail. He or she also needs a dictionary of literary terms and a dictionary of quotations. All three types of dictionary are indispensable. The following can be recommended:

Abrams, M. H.: *A Glossary of Literary Terms*, third edition (New York, Holt Rinehart & Wiston, 1971).

Barnhart, C. L. (ed.): *The American College Dictionary* (New York, Random House, 1963).

Cohen, J. M. & M. J.: *The Penguin Dictionary of Quotations* (Harmondsworth, Penguin Books, 1960).

Other Works

The most useful books for readers who wish to go further into the topics I have raised are those which discuss important concepts, and those which contain good examples of detailed discussion of particular passages of poetry, drama, and prose fiction.

The following handbooks do both these things at a fairly simple level:

(a)

Brooks, C. & Heilman, R. B.: *Understanding Drama* (New York, Henry Holt, 1945).

Brooks, C. & Warren, R. P.: *Understanding Fiction* (New York, Appleton-Century-Crofts, 1943).

Brooks, C. & Warren, R. P.: *Understanding Poetry* (New York, Henry Holt, 1950).

Cox, C. B. & Dyson, A. E.: *The Practical Criticism of Poetry: a textbook* (London, Arnold, 1965).

Cross, K. G. W. & Marsh, D. R. C.: *Poetry Reading and Understanding* (Melbourne, Cheshire, 1966).

Main, C. F. & Seng, P. J.: *Poems* (Belmont, Wadsworth, 1961).

Rawlinson, D. H.: *The Practice of Criticism* (Cambridge, Cambridge University Press, 1968).
Rosenthal, M. L. & Smith, A. J. M.: *Exploring Poetry* (New York, Macmillan, 1955).

(b) Particular concepts are discussed at a more advanced level in the *Critical Idiom* series published by Methuen & Co. The following are particularly useful in connection with topics discussed in this book: *Irony* (D. C. Muecke), *Metaphor* (Terence Hawkes), *Rhetoric* (Peter Dixon), *Satire* (Arthur Pollard). Each volume also contains a helpful bibliography.

(c) The following three books contain excellent detailed discussions of particular passages of literary writing, at a considerably advanced level:

Lodge, David: *The Language of Fiction* (London, Routledge & Kegan Paul, 1966).
Nowottny, Winifred: *The Language Poets Use* (London, Athlone Press, 1962).
Styan, J. L.: *The Dramatic Experience: A Guide to the Reading of Plays* (London, Cambridge University Press, 1965).

(d) Finally, the following contain excellent extended discussions of particular concepts, at a highly advanced level:

Davie, Donald: *Articulate Energy: An Enquiry into the Syntax of English Poetry* (London, Routledge & Kegan Paul, 1955).
Davis, R. M. (ed.): *The Novel: Modern Essays in Criticism* (Englewood Cliffs, Prentice-Hall, 1969). *Contains important essays on narrative point of view by Norman Friedman and Wayne C. Booth.*
Muecke, D. C.: *The Compass of Irony* (London, Methuen, 1969).
Pope, Alexander: *Peri Bathous: Or the Art of Sinking in Poetry*, 1727; reprinted in *Alexander Pope: Selected Poetry and Prose*, edited by W. K. Wimsatt (New York, Rinehart, 1951). *An ironic treatise on the best ways for poets to produce bathos.*
Vickers, Brian: *Classical Rhetoric in English Poetry* (London, Macmillan, 1970). *Invaluable for figurative language and patterns of syntax.*

11
Index of Terms

The following list includes neither the major terms used as chapter-headings, nor those included under 'Additional Terms'. Taken together with these, the following make up an essential minimum of terms which the student needs to be familiar with.

alliteration 86
antithesis 86, 87
authorial intrusion(s) 31–2
black comedy 74–5
connotation(s) 4–6
decorum 25
denotation(s) 4
direct interior monologue 34,
    52–3
direct speech 33
distance 35–6, 61, 86–7, 90
dramatic monologue 31, 51–2
elevated diction 7–8
end-stopped lines 88–9
epic poetry 90, 97
epistolary novel 32, 55
evaluative words 4–5, 8–9
evaluative figures of comparison
    21, 22–4
first-person narratives 31
foregrounded style 89–90
Gothic novel 97
Horatian satire 73

indirect speech 33
ironic comments 55–7
ironic impersonations 48–55
ironic situations 47–8, 57, 59
Juvenalian satire 73
metaphors 19
mock-heroic poetry 97–9
narrated interior monologue 34,
    53–5, 90
parallel(ism) 85, 87
paraphrased speech 33
paraphrased thought 34–5
parody 55, 73
personifications 19–20
reported speech 33
run-on lines 88–9
satire 73
sensory imagery 16–17
serio-comic writing 72
similes 18
symbol 21–2
syntax 84–7, 89, 90
third-person narratives 31